Master

Presenter

Master
Presenter

Lessons from the World's Top Experts on
Becoming a More Influential Speaker

The Best of PresentationXpert

David Zielinski

Editor

WILEY

Published by Wiley.

A Wiley Brand

One Montgomery Street, Suite 1200, San Francisco, CA 94104-4594

www.wiley.com

For additional copies/bulk purchases of this book in the U.S. please contact 800-274-4434.

Wiley books and products are available through most bookstores. To contact Wiley directly call our Customer Care Department within the U.S. at 800-274-4434, outside the U.S. at 317-572-3985, fax 317-572-4002, or visit www.wiley.com.

Wiley publishes in a variety of print and electronic formats and by print-on-demand. Some material included with standard print versions of this book may not be included in e-books or in print-on-demand. If this book refers to media such as a CD or DVD that is not included in the version you purchased, you may download this material at http://booksupport.wiley.com. For more information about Wiley products, visit www.wiley.com.

Library of Congress Cataloging-in-Publication Data

Master presenter : Lessons from the world's top experts on becoming a more influential speaker / David Zielinski, editor.
    pages cm
  Includes index.
  ISBN 978-1-118-48588-0 (paper/website); ISBN 978-1-118-65441-5 (ebk.); ISBN 978-1-118-65458-3 (ebk.); ISBN 978-1-118-65459-0 (ebk.) 1. Business presentations. I. Zielinski, David editor of compilation.
  HF5718.22.M326 2013
  658.4'51—dc23

                                            2013011648

Printed in the United States of America

PB Printing   10~NS9~NS8~NS7~NS6~NS5~NS4~NS3~NS2~NS1

CONTENTS

FOREWORD

N O ONE ASPIRES TO be average.

But for the millions of people every day who find themselves trying to present information and ideas to others, the path seems littered with countless examples of those who have settled for "just getting by." They run from meeting to meeting, plane to plane, conference to conference, and over time have abdicated the exceptional for the mundane in this most personal of all business communication processes—the art of presenting.

And this challenge today is not simply the domain of small companies that just don't know any better. We see the impact on organizations of all shapes and sizes. As employees watch their senior leaders fill their presentation screens full of mind-numbing content, or see managers who make little eye contact with audiences and recite bullet points verbatim from text-dense slides, a lowered bar of expectations is handed down to all of us like a winter coat in a large family.

Delivering a presentation will always be a very personal thing.

And that seems to be the ultimate challenge in any discussion around the art of presenting. There will always be a very real connection between mediocrity in presenting and its consequences. Careers will fall short of what they could have been. Employees might entrench in their indifference after a CEO's overly detailed message and weak delivery. Partners will fail to catch a vision for a new idea. And far too often, the very best idea in the room will never see the light of day. There are always consequences.

So it would seem that being a good communicator today is not something we can simply dabble in if we have a little extra time. It will always be one of those life skills, like balancing our checkbooks, that will impact our lives well beyond our immediate understanding. So if we can all agree at some level on this simple truth, what's the problem? Too often today the challenge seems to be finding the kind of resources that strike a balance between time invested and observable change in what we do and how we do it.

But very fortunately for all of us who present, from time to time people come along who offer a unique vantage point. They've been around long enough to have seen software come and go and technologies evolve. They understand the tips and ideas that have been validated through the test of time and know rock-solid best practices constantly bubble to the top. And for me, that's what Dave Zielinski brings to any discussion on presenting.

For those of us who have been reading his presentation-related articles for nearly two decades, we know it's not just a writing assignment. It's part of his own personal exploration, and he invites us along on the discovery. And even today, he continues to set himself apart as one who has studied the art from the inside out and makes it easy for his readers to walk away with something actionable—not simply theoretical.

In this, Dave's most recent book, he distills out for you the best-of-the-best insight gleaned from years as a writer and editor and pulls together in one place ideas from those he's collaborated with through the years. But what I like most is that you don't have to dedicate a long weekend to mining out the nuggets. In every chapter, you'll find a rich depth of advice from experts who have spent a lifetime working with those who create and deliver presentations. Need a fresh approach to shape your message for next month's leadership event? There's a chapter for that. Tired of visuals that still look like they did a decade ago? He has an answer for you here. Looking for a few delivery skills to help you get through tomorrow's big presentation with a little extra confidence? He has a chapter for that, too.

You see, being an average presenter is actually pretty easy these days. Presenters can simply do what they've always done before. They can fall back into old habits and keep the bar comfortably low for themselves and for those around them.

But if you aspire to be the type of presenter people remember—the one who stands out at the end of a very long day and whose ideas are remembered long after your audiences dive back into their very busy lives—don't miss this engaging read!

Never be average again.

Jim Endicott, President

Distinction Communication Inc.

ACKNOWLEDGEMENTS

THIS BOOK WOULD NOT exist without the generous contributions and permissions of the world-class presentation skill coaches, trainers, and experts who regularly write for *PresentationXpert* newsletter. The list of those I'd like to thank for lending their wisdom and lessons learned to the book includes, in no order of importance: Jim Endicott, Rick Altman, Ellen Finkelstein, Dianna Booher, Dave Paradi, Mike Parkinson, Geetesh Bajaj, Robert Lane, Tom Mucciolo, Nancy Duarte, Cliff Atkinson, Lisa B. Marshall, Peter Cohan, Patricia Fripp, David Green, Doug Stevenson, Olivia Mitchell, Ben Decker, Marjorie Brody, John Billington, Angela DeFinis, T.J. Walker, Greg Owen-Boger, Steve Mandel, Sue Hershkowitz-Coore, and Jeremey Donovan.

A big thank you also is in order to Keely Vazquez and Paul Kolars, the managing partners of TriMax Direct, the company that publishes *PresentationXpert* newsletter, for their support and encouragement of this project. Finally, I'd like to thank Matt Davis of Wiley for seeing the potential in the book and his colleagues Ryan Noll and Michael Kay for so capably overseeing manuscript editing and production.

Dave Zielinski
April 2013

INTRODUCTION

THE ACT OF GETTING UP to speak before an audience has long ranked near the top of people's greatest fears in life. While that may still be the case, we think it's high time for another take on that age-old belief, particularly as it applies to business presenting.

Butterflies or healthy anticipation is one thing, fear quite another. Presenting offers a golden opportunity for businesspeople to take their own careers—and their company's success—to another level. It represents one of the few times in a work life when the spotlight shines solely on you, allowing others to benefit from your hard-won knowledge or insight.

While many may find that intimidating, we hope more begin to see it as liberating and embrace the challenge. We think the act of presenting should be welcomed and relished, and no longer lumped in with death, taxes, or trips to the dentist.

After all, how we perceive a future event greatly influences how well we perform once that moment arrives.

Why a Need for This Book?

Survey after survey shows that most businesspeople believe their presentation skills affect their career progress and income level. But the not-so-good news is that surveys also indicate a considerable gap between how good people think their own presentation skills are and the differing views of those in their audience.

In short, the mass of businesspeople—whether unknowingly or consciously—settle for "just getting by" as presenters, and mediocrity now seems an acceptable standard in the field. That's troubling, because the stakes associated with developing and delivering high-impact presentations are higher than ever.

Whether it's a salesperson delivering a PowerPoint pitch to capture a contract pursued by a bevy of global competitors, a manager speaking via webcast to rally troops who've just experienced a downsizing or poor quarter, or a hallway conversation with an influential colleague about a new product idea, how effective people are at presenting their ideas is as close to a universally critical business skill as exists today.

Presenting also is one of the most difficult business skills to master, demanding a combination of interpersonal, graphic design, and technical competence uncommon to many disciplines.

Consider the repertoire of skills required. Most presenters are far from PowerPoint specialists or graphic design experts—their expertise instead resting in areas like sales, management, or human resources—yet need much more than a "weekend warrior's" knowledge of design software to create professional-looking slides or graphics. They also need a market researcher's keen insight in order to craft key messages and select supporting data targeted to an audience's unique needs. Finally, they must be skilled communicators to deliver those messages in a clear, credible, and compelling fashion.

Today's presenters also have to accomplish all of this amid absurdly busy work schedules, a result of leaner organizational workforces that are likely to persist into the foreseeable future. They have to find time to develop speaking scripts, customize PowerPoint slides, master new presenting technologies, and rehearse delivery when many other daily work duties are calling their names.

How This Book Addresses Reader Needs

That's where the *Master Presenter* comes in. This book features the collective wisdom, real-world experiences, and lessons learned of some of the world's top presentation skill coaches, most of whom are regular contributors to *PresentationXpert* e-newsletter, a monthly publication from TriMax Direct in St. Paul, Minnesota.

Master Presenter was created with the time-starved business presenter in mind. The book's collection of short, highly practical articles offers take-away ideas, insider tips, and how-to advice we hope readers can immediately put to use to improve the design or delivery of their presentations. The information applies whether you are speaking in person to large audiences, presenting via the web, or using a hand-held presentations device to inform, educate, or persuade small groups.

Rather than asking you to cut through the underbrush of long chapters to find information relevant to your needs, our goal is to help you quickly scan in-chapter headlines, article subheads, or bullet points to zero in on content that appeals to you.

The book is written for salespeople, corporate trainers, human resource professionals, executives, managers, corporate communicators, and other businesspeople who frequently design or deliver presentations, but who likely don't consider themselves experts in use of slide design software, graphics creation, or storytelling. While delivering effective presentations is vital to their success, it is only one of many skills they must master to perform their jobs at high levels.

The book's content is crafted for the real world, where the realities of corporate life often stand in the way of aspirations like developing visually stunning PowerPoint slides or conducting multiple rehearsals before a presentation. Our goal is to help you achieve presentations excellence within tight time frames, in team environments, and amid the sometimes-daunting demands of clients.

Rather than reflecting the world view or experiences of a sole presentation skills trainer or consultant, *Master Presenter* features carefully selected wisdom and practical tips from a variety of seasoned presentation skill coaches. We aim to leave few stones unturned in offering perspectives, ideas, or lessons learned that can help you become a better presenter.

How This Book Is Organized

Here is a look at how this book is organized to help guide you through your journey:

Chapter 1: Creating the Presentation Blueprint. Developing the proper mix and flow of key messages, data, slide narration, and personal stories is the key to good presentation planning, but not easily achieved. This chapter provides expert tips and guidelines for how to create a good presentation blueprint, without which a memorable presentation is not possible.

Chapter 2: What's in It for Them? Developing Audience-Centric Messages. Presenters too often create content from their own eyes or a company's perspective, rather than from the viewpoint of audiences. No one likes to be dragged through sixty minutes of material than only touches on ten minutes of their relevant need. Self-serving messages are a death knell for any presentation. Here we provide strategies and tips for how to shape messages and choose supporting data that is focused on an audience's "pain points."

Chapter 3: Perfect Practice: Maximizing Your Rehearsal Time. One of the busy presenter's most common complaints is "no time for rehearsal." Knowing how to use limited rehearsal time shrewdly can make the difference between a presentation that soars and one that never gets off the ground. This chapter covers the important difference between practice and rehearsal and offers ideas for how to obtain the most from short rehearsal periods.

Chapter 4: Tapping PowerPoint's Hidden Potential. Microsoft's PowerPoint software has plenty of fans as well as foes, but its effectiveness ultimately lies in how it's used and in mastering some of the software's little-known features. Deploy it like a poor-man's teleprompter—designing slides weighed down with wordy bullet points and then reading that text verbatim—and your audiences will tune out. But use text sparingly, and employ headlines, graphics, or photos deftly on slides, and PowerPoint can increase audience attention while boosting message retention.

Here we provide slide design ideas, insider shortcuts, and tips to help you use PowerPoint's latest versions in ways that enable the software to live up to its often-unfulfilled promise.

Chapter 5: Graphics Design for the Non-Graphics Professional. Most PowerPoint users aren't graphic design experts; their expertise instead resting in sales or marketing, management, corporate training, or communications. The ideas and tips in this chapter will help the non-graphic design professional become more proficient at creating professional-looking, high-impact slide graphics in shorter time frames.

Chapter 6: Mastering New Presentation Media: Webinars, Mobile Presenting, and Social Media. It's becoming just as common for businesspeople to deliver presentations over the web or using mobile devices like iPads as it is to use a standard projector-and-laptop setup in face-to-face settings. In this chapter our experts offer advice for how to adapt your presentation design or delivery skills in ways that help you thrive when using these new mediums.

Chapter 7: The Art of Persuasion: How Influence Really Happens During Presentations. There are plenty of misconceptions about how influence happens in the presentations arena, and this chapter separates myth from reality when it comes to the art of persuasion. Our experts provide a host of proven, research-based techniques to help you improve your personal influence as a presenter, a skill no speaker can do without.

Chapter 8: Winning the Pitch: Delivering Effective Sales Presentations. Delivering winning sales presentations not only requires good technical presenting skills, it also demands presenters understand human psychology and be able to mind-read prospects in their audience. More sales presentations and product demos are occurring in new mediums, requiring new design and delivery skills. This chapter provides expert advice and from-the-trenches lessons from those who've been on the winning side of high-stakes sales pitches.

Chapter 9: The Power of Story: Honing Your Storytelling Skills. Audiences remember a brief, well-told story much longer than bullet points on a slide or data in a bar graph, and stories connected to key messages impact audiences on emotional levels in ways facts or studies never can. But like any skill, good storytelling requires study and repeated practice to achieve mastery. This chapter will help even presenters who don't consider themselves natural storytellers to begin spinning better, more memorable tales for their audiences.

Chapter 10: Tuning the Speaking Instruments: Body Language, Vocal Techniques, and Eye Contact. The "how" of delivering presentation messages is often overshadowed by the "what" of developing PowerPoint slide content. This chapter explores how use of body language, eye contact, and vocal techniques influences your impact as a presenter. It also provides how-to tips for using those speaking "instruments" in ways that ensure the quality of your delivery matches the quality of your content.

Chapter 11: Disaster Recovery: Managing Challenging Presentation Situations. Regardless of how well you prepare for presentations, something will eventually go wrong, often at the worst possible time. It might be a technology meltdown, a memory lapse while speaking, or a disruptive audience member. How well you steal victory from the jaws of defeat in these trying situations has a big impact on how audiences view your credibility and effectiveness as a presenter.

This chapter provides a host of proven tactics for how to cope when Mr. Murphy inevitably rears his head in your presentations room.

Dave Zielinski
April 2013

1

Creating the Presentation Blueprint

A noted presentation skills coach is fond of saying that "most planes crash on take-offs and landings—and so do most presentations." The failure to plan correctly—to create a well-conceived presentation *blueprint* or script for your opening, body, and close—is one of the biggest reasons that presentations veer off the runway.

When asked in a recent survey by a leading presentation consulting firm what their biggest presentations' challenge was, a majority of corporate presenters said "putting together a good message so my presentation connects and flows well."

Achieving the proper flow of data, personal stories, and humor—and ensuring main messages are tailored to the audience's "pain points"—are the keys to good presentation planning. This chapter contains tips and insights to help you on the journey toward creating better blueprints.

• • •

PRESENTING WITH IMPACT: HOW TO CRAFT A MEMORABLE MESSAGE
Dianna Booher

EXCUSE ME FOR PARAPHRASING a cliché, but you are what you write and say. Your reputation with customers or business colleagues often rests on a single interaction. Whether presenting in a boardroom or conducting daily business, you may only have one shot at communicating—not just your message, but who you are.

So What's Your Point?

You do have one, right? And a purpose? In any communication—whether a speech, e-mail, report, meeting, cafeteria poster, or trade show hospitality suite—identify your purpose: Is it to inform, persuade, inspire, coach, commend, warn, entertain, introduce, overcome objections, respond to concerns, or answer questions?

Once you've determined your real purpose, you can shape your one-sentence message as a road map.

Take a Point of View

Avoid hype as a form of persuasion. But remember that the absence of hype doesn't mean the absence of opinion.

Hired to help an investment company develop and shape their message, I listened to four executive vice presidents as they presented their segments of the "official" company overview. The general counsel presented his overview of real estate investing and new regulatory laws relating to such.

When he finished, I asked him, "Do you think real estate is a good investment for high-net-worth individuals today?"

"Absolutely," he said. "The best. For several reasons." And he listed them for me.

"Why didn't you include those reasons in your presentation?" I asked.

"I did."

"I missed them."

"Maybe they didn't come across as reasons. But the facts were there. The investor could have drawn that conclusion."

"But why would you leave it to the listener to draw that conclusion?"

"Well, I'm a lawyer. I didn't want to come across as a used car salesman."

For the next hour, we discussed the differences between hype and a persuasive presentation. After all, his organization spent several million dollars annually flying in estate planners, financial advisors, brokers, and potential clients to persuade them to invest in real estate.

Why would he not want to lead them to a conclusion?

Be clear about your purpose. If you're asked just to dump information, do it. *But more often than not, you're expected to take a point of view about the information you provide.* That point of view involves the four S's of persuasion to make sure all your listeners arrive at the same destination: solid facts, sound logic, straightforward language, and strong structure.

Translate Concepts Like "Vision," "Strategy," and "Initiatives" to Specifics

If you're speaking to an audience larger than one and using these vague terms, people are going to have different tasks in mind for their next week's to-do list. Vision in Asian corporations often refers to plans to be executed twenty to fifty years into the future, while vision in American companies may refer to the next quarter.

It's not just the lower-ranking employees you address who'll want more specifics. Political candidates receive as much criticism for vagueness on implementing their campaign promises as they do for their positions on controversial issues. *People demand the particulars.*

Remember That Facts Aren't Reasons

Have you ever researched a "fact" on the Internet and found contradictory data?

For example: The Family Life Communications research firm has said that the average U.S. household spends $490 each year on Christmas gifts. The National Retail Federation reports that the average consumer spends $738 on holiday gifts. MOPS (Mothers of Preschoolers) says that the average household spends over $1,000 for gifts during the holidays.

The fact is that facts can be false, wrong, misleading, or misinterpreted—purposefully or accidentally. Even if a fact happens to be correct, it doesn't always double as a reason.

For example, a salesperson may tell me that I can buy a caseload of off-brand PDAs for a special price of $99 each to give to key clients as a gift at the end of the year to express appreciation for their business.

The salesperson may interpret that fact as a reason to make the purchase: a low price, a nice gift for clients. I may interpret that same fact as a reason *not* to make the purchase. No matter the special price, giving an off-brand to key clients may not create a good impression and instead may make my company look cheap.

Facts are just facts, until you interpret them as reasons "for" or "against" something.

Make Your Facts Tell a Story

To be useful, facts have to serve some sort of strategy. The only thing worse than filling up your speech, slides, e-mails, or reports with fact after fact after fact . . . is not shaping them to tell your story.

What story do your facts tell? What trail do the facts leave?

Tell how your division exploded with the introduction of the new widget, and your headcount climbed from three to sixty-eight engineers in the first two years you were in business. Then tell how you grew lax in your quality control. Tell about your reject rates.

Show how the customer satisfaction numbers plummeted. Show how orders started dropping off as fast as they were logged onto the computer. Then circle back to the layoff of fifty-eight engineers three years later.

Then out of the ashes came. . . . Well, you get the picture.

Drama. Dialogue. Climax. Denouement

Set the scene at the trade show. How many competitors were there? How many attendees? Of those, how many did your booth attract? Why? What was the attraction—or non-attraction? What did the competitor do to drive you nuts? What kind of lead follow-up/closing ratio do you have to do after the trade show to make your competitors eat dust?

Music, lights, camera, action. Facts alone will never feed the mind—at least not for long.

Analogy and Metaphor: Juicy Details Deliver Big Impact

Analogies lead to a conclusion based on a specific comparison and add significant impact to a factual argument.

Jeff Bezos, founder and CEO of Amazon.com, used this analogy in a report to shareholders: "Long-term thinking is both a requirement and an outcome of true ownership. Owners are different from tenants. I know of a couple who rented out their house and the family who moved in nailed their Christmas tree to the hardwood floors instead of using a tree stand. Expedient, I suppose, and admittedly these were particularly bad tenants, but no owner would be so short-sighted. Similarly, many investors are effectively short-term tenants, turning their portfolios over so quickly they are really just renting the stocks that they temporarily 'own.' "

We talk about "prime real estate" in referring to the home page of a website or placement above the fold in a newspaper or product catalog. Many human resource managers talk about "cafeteria" benefits to their employees. With just one word, this analogy implies that employees have a "menu" of benefits to select from, that a "parent" has agreed to cover the "total" invoice up to a certain amount, that employees select according to "taste or preferences" from that menu.

Such comparisons as these don't exactly solicit an emotional response; they simply clarify a complex concept.

Metaphors, on the other hand, imply a comparison and typically evoke an emotion and a mindset. Both types of comparisons can be succinct, yet powerful ways to manage how people think about an idea or situation.

If you wanted to make the point that someone was not fully engaged with his or her colleagues in a mission, you might use a war metaphor: "John ducks into his cubicle as if it were a foxhole. He needs to stick his head out occasionally and help the rest of us fight the war. Otherwise, the parent company is going to take over the entire department."

If you wanted to talk about how indifference to quality customer service could destroy your business, you might put it in these terms: "Our poor customer service has become a *cancer* eating away at our business. I see customers walk in here and wait ten minutes before being greeted. Then once we do help them locate what they need in the store, they have to wait again at the checkout. Then they wait again at the loading dock. The longer a customer stays in our store, it's like our cancer metastasizes rather than goes into remission."

Author Malcolm Gladwell uses the metaphor of "contagious disease" in his bestseller *The Tipping Point* to describe how ideas gradually "catch on" and spread in the general population.

Metaphors and analogies, by their very selection, create a powerful way of thinking about an issue and often evoke a strong accompanying emotion that makes ideas memorable.

Truth That Tells, Truth That Sells

When presenting an agenda, giving a speech, or trying to illustrate a point, actual experiences can be as strong as cold fact.

Whatever your message, stories will make it stronger: courage, determination, commitment, persistence, customer service, vision, caution, change. Consider all the stories that have created the rich cultures and legendary CEOs. There's the story about the employee who made a costly mistake at IBM that cost the company $10,000, then walked into CEO Tom Watson's office to offer his resignation.

Watson's famous line: "Why would I want your resignation? I just paid $10,000 for your education."

Such culture-creating stories still surface during my consulting projects. Perry, a financial advisor and now regional manager of a large brokerage house, encourages his trainees to use more stories in their sales presentations with clients by telling his own story of an earlier lost account.

He was competing with another brokerage house for the 401(k) funds at a large hospital system in the Northeast. The hospital invited him and a competitor in to make a presentation to the group of employees, after which the employees could choose where to invest their 401(k) funds.

Perry walked in with all the facts on his side—better yields, better customer service ratings, wider fund choices, more flexibility in the plans. His competitor walked in with a better presentation. She focused on a few stories of how her company got involved in the lives of their clients, helping them to achieve their personal goals, particularly in times of crisis.

She walked away with 92 percent of the employee accounts; Perry, 8 percent. He attributed the loss solely to his competitor's use of stories to make her points memorable.

Drive your point home with a well-chosen story. On the other hand, *never use a $100 story in a three-minute time slot to make a nickel point.* Make sure the point deserves a story.

Consider carefully as you develop your presentation message. If your goal is retention and impact, create, shape, and deliver accordingly—with the finishing touches that pack a wallop.

Dianna Booher is the CEO of Booher Consultants (www.booher.com) in Dallas, Texas, and works with organizations to increase their productivity and effectiveness through better oral, written, interpersonal, and cross-functional communication.

• • •

SIX TIPS FOR CREATING POWERFUL PRESENTATION SCRIPTS
Tom Mucciolo

HERE ARE A FEW tips for creating a more effective story or *script*, or one that allows you to control the flow of your presentation message using a well-thought-out pattern.

1. Structuring a Script

No matter which way you choose to present the information, you still have to develop a pattern or a structure to the script so the information can be absorbed properly. Think of the structure as a type of script that is used to convey the message.

Most presentations follow a linear pattern that moves from an opening through the body and, finally, into the closing. Like any movie or book, there is an expectation to have the anchors of a beginning, middle, and end.

This *open-body-close* process is very common and usually expected as the metaphor for receiving information. Regardless of the type of script you create, the audience is preconditioned to accept a linear pattern, the end of which includes some closure (call to action).

If the opening and closing parts of the script mostly tap emotions, then, for balance, the *body* should mostly tap the intellect. Since the body of the message is filled mainly with facts, we also need to add some feelings (such as stories) to avoid a massive data dump.

It is the *timely* mix of facts and feelings, spread over the *open-body-close* pattern, which allows the message to create a lasting impression.

2. Micro-to-Macro Scripting

In a presentation you usually separate the *macro* items (market data, trends, company information, and competition) from the *micro* items (stories, analogies, specific examples, features, and benefits).

Although the big picture is usually chosen as the starting point for a script, the small details are the qualifiers of the argument. Because time is an issue to a listener, *getting to the details is more critical than hearing about the general trends.*

For example, you would obviously prefer to know whether the route you take to work is clear before you care to know that your city is the eighth-most-traffic-congested in the country. When a script is constructed in a *micro-to-macro* fashion, the *unique* issues you bring to the table are discussed first and the broad-based marketing data is secondary.

The good news is that if you accidentally run out of time in the presentation, the audience only misses the general information. Chances are, they can find that data whenever they choose.

3. Matching Ideals

This script structure is really a set-up for the audience. The strategy is that you describe the ideal product or service, which you already know will closely resemble your own product or service.

Since the audience accepts your description as the premise for the argument, it is quite easy to match your argument to the premise you set up in the first place.

This structure is usually used more for products than for services, since attributes of a product are more tangible (visible) than qualities of a service.

For example, you selectively mention the ideal attributes of a good car. You say, *"The ideal car has front-wheel drive, dual air bags, a rear defrost, and a trunk release."*

By setting this premise, you naturally gain the audience's agreement that these are the ideal attributes of a good car. Then you describe your car in terms of the ideal, making sure you only compare to about 90 percent of the ideal.

You say, *"OUR car has front-wheel drive, dual air bags, a rear defrost, BUT we're still working on the trunk release."*

You never want to compare to 100 percent because that would mean you have the perfect product (which no one does), and it would leave you no room for improvement. After all, how do you improve on perfection?

The matching ideals script is designed to lead the audience to believe that the product (or service) is the *best* one for the job, but it may not do the *whole job*. This leaves you an open-ended reason for later updates and improvements.

4. Main Points

Typically, this script is used with information-based presentations such as those dealing with financial results and other historical data. The process follows the time-honored pattern:

Tell 'em what you're gonna tell 'em.

Tell 'em.

Tell 'em what you just told 'em.

One way to identify this structure is the appearance of an *agenda* early in the presentation and a corresponding summary at the end. This lets the audience know what to expect and then anticipate what to remember. The summary at the end is critical because main points can be hard to remember, especially when many supporting points are discussed.

The audience may get lost unless it is constantly made aware of how the supporting information relates to the main points. If you limit the number of main points and supporting points, the recall process will be easier for the audience.

5. Question and Answer

Question-and-answer scripting is similar to the corporate training activity of pre-testing and post-testing. This is useful in training sessions when a lot of unrelated, yet comprehensive information must be covered.

First, you *pre-test* the audience's knowledge of a subject using easy-to-answer questions (true/false, multiple choice, etc.). The questions cover all the major points you expect to convey. Then, during the session, you reveal the correct answers using supporting visual elements to explain each answer as you elaborate. Finally, you ask the audience as a group to answer the original questions (post-test).

A question-answer scripting structure can be used in a variety of presentation situations, including surveys, polls, and research studies. The objective should address how the information will be used by the audience to achieve a particular result.

One way to ensure that the information is more than just a data dump is to repeat key points and summarize conclusions at several stages of the presentation.

6. Problem-Solution

Also known as the *divide and conquer* script, the problem-solution structure is one of the most effective scripts. It is especially useful for high-level, decision-oriented presentations. The problem-solution script can concentrate either on mistakes or on missed opportunities.

If the script focuses on failures, it accentuates the negative. If it points out overlooked potential, it stresses the positive. Either approach leaves the door open for a hero to save the day.

The process follows a simple pattern. First, the overall problem is described and presented in a manner that makes it look positive (or negative). Then, you dissect the problem into smaller sections that can be addressed individually.

Finally, the solutions to the smaller areas will solve the big problem, as well. Whether you focus on the negative or the positive aspects of the problem, the result of the script (the solution) will *always look positive.*

Every presentation is based on a line of logic or reason for imparting the information. When you structure the data according to a consistent pattern, the audience is better able to follow your discussion and remain focused throughout your talk. And that's the whole story!

Tom Mucciolo is president of MediaNet Inc. (www.medianet-ny.com/), a presentation skills consulting company in New York City specializing in the design and delivery of electronic presentations.

• • •

USE UNEXPECTED OPENERS TO CAPTURE AUDIENCE INTEREST
David Green

THE INFORMAL NETWORKING SESSION was over and the twenty-odd working speechwriters took their seats in the conference room in eager anticipation of the lunch speaker. It was to be Ted Sorenson, renowned speechwriter and confidante for John F. Kennedy during his White House years.

Sorenson took his place at the podium, smiled kindly at the gathering, and then began: "Thank you so much for having me here today. It is quite an honor to be with you . . . *and that concludes my prepared remarks."*

Now, if you are a god in your industry and have the audience hanging on your every word before you even open your mouth, you can get away with an opening like that. But when it comes to making speeches and presentations, most of us are still mere mortals. And, as the saying goes, you have only one chance to make a first impression. So your opening comments are critical. You have to engage your audience from the get-go.

That's why so many speakers think they need to start their talks with a story or a joke to "get the audience on their side." These opening gambits are what I call "speech props" and they can be extremely useful . . . in concept.

But not if they come from one of those "five hundred great jokes for public speakers" sourcebooks.

Because you not only have to engage your audience, you have to overcome their expectations so that they don't write you off before you get to the good stuff in your presentation. Oh yes, the audience thinks they know what to expect from you. They know your title, your company, maybe they've seen an abstract—they think they have you pegged.

Power of the Unexpected

So it's time to counter-program by opening with a story that throws them off balance, that bends their perspective, that makes them look at you with fresh eyes . . . and listen with fresh ears.

This is pure Made-to-Stick 101—and if that reference doesn't ring a bell, you might want to check out Chip and Dan Heath's book *Made to Stick: Why Some Ideas Survive and Others Die.*

The Heath brothers offer six basic precepts for creating memorable communications, but the one I particularly fancy is Principle 2: Unexpectedness. Here's their take on why unexpectedness matters:

> "*How do we get our audience to pay attention to our ideas, and how do we maintain their interest when we need time to*

get the ideas across? We need to violate people's expectations.
We need to be counterintuitive."

Okay, fine . . . so how do you do that exactly? By following these
three basic "rules."

1. Look Outside the Box

Get outside your industry. Look for stimuli that aren't "making the
rounds." Seek provocative thinking. One of the best sources might
be the website of the Technology, Entertainment, and Design (TED)
conference, www.ted.com. Many of the five- to twenty-minute talks
posted there, videotaped from the conference proceedings, are
highly effective at turning your head around and making you see
your world differently.

I have a friend who, knowing that I do a lot of work with technology companies, occasionally sends me articles like "The ten
stupidest tech company blunders" with the note "good anecdotes
for speeches."

But you'll often find that the best anecdotes for speeches are
the ones that come from out of left field. These tend to engage
the audience more as they try to figure out where you are going.
For example, in recent speeches and ghosted columns for an
art-education association client, I've used these topics:

- The doctrine of the Cluetrain Manifesto

- Bud Clark's stunning mayoral win in Portland, Oregon, in
  1984

- The fact that Minneapolis and St. Paul aren't entirely on
  opposite banks of the Mississippi

How could such a hodge-podge of disparate and arcane leads
make sense? Well, since the association was going through a major
cultural transformation, my client's first task was to capture her
membership's attention. Then she needed to champion her cause—
over a period of time—enlisting passionate support, and creating
local champions to spread the gospel.

So the Cluetrain Manifesto, which advocates for digital media's ability to overcome the stranglehold of corporate-speak, introduced the power of authenticity in an individual's voice.

The Minneapolis-St. Paul geographic trivia reference was the intro to a speech she gave in Minneapolis—and was used as an example of how preconceptions based on conventional wisdom can keep us from our goals.

Bud Clark's mayoral win, which I knew about from living in Portland shortly before that election, was a model for harnessing populist fervor to overcome great odds.

Dramatically different leads, but all working on the same wavelength to effectively empower the association's members to take a more activist role.

2. Let Inspiration Come to You

Many years ago, when I was working as an advertising copywriter in New York City, I told my boss that the company should just pay me to walk back and forth between the subway station and the office because I had more good ideas during those thirty minutes—when I wasn't really trying—than in the eight hours a day I spent at my desk.

A few months ago, a client told me that she loved receiving e-mails from me that start out "I was just out for a walk along the reservoir and I got to thinking. . . ." The best ideas are like that squiggly dust mote on your eye that you catch a fleeting glance of when you gaze up into a summer sky, but that darts out of sight when you try to look directly at it.

The more you expose yourself to influences outside your industry, the more you open yourself up to cross-pollination, which is where creativity is most often born. For instance, I once found the conceptual construct for a speech on complexity versus simplicity in the midst of watching the movie *Pollock*.

Watching Pollock's chaotic jumble of splatter painting seemed to represent technological complexity in a very obvious way. Later, for stark contrast, I chose Mark Rothko's tranquil works, with their blocks of muted color, to represent simplicity. The speech was by the CEO of a networking equipment company to industry analysts and angel investors and, after a brief scene-setting comment about the challenge of developing breakthrough innovation, he got into his true lead:

> "So every now and again, I like to look at our challenge from an entirely different frame of reference. It keeps me fresh. And I'm willing to bet that it will make the next twenty-five minutes [show Jackson Pollock slide] more intriguing than maybe you thought they were going to be.
>
> "I figured I could get away with using Jackson Pollock as my keynote visual, because you're all eclectic, multi-dimensional people, with diverse interests. If I tried this with an engineering audience, I'd probably lose the entire audience while they scribbled down all the architectural flaws in Pollock's schematic.
>
> "Now, I'm a network guy. I look at Jackson Pollock and I see networks. Specifically, I see today's wide area networks—the complexity, the layers, the obstacles to flow. Of course, if you know anything about Jackson Pollock as a person, you know that he was a bona-fide tortured soul, which I suspect might eventually describe the engineers in charge of building broadband networks on [complex] SONET-based architecture.
>
> [switch to Mark Rothko slide]
>
> "Now, Mark Rothko—he's my idea of an Ethernet Everywhere guy. There's a fundamental simplicity here, and a sense of the infinite—infinite space, infinite potential."

3. Practice Storytelling

This may seem like splitting hairs, but there really is a difference between *storytelling* and *telling a story*. Storytelling is about more than the relating of an anecdote; it's about the creation of a distinctive, intriguingly listenable voice.

Let me give you an example. I had a technology client who wanted to build a keynote address around the message that his industry needed radical innovation in order to jump-start recovery from the 2001 recession. The tepid, incremental, more-bang-for-your-buck product improvements that had dominated the recession period no longer would accomplish the job.

While the speech was still in incubator mode, I came across an article about building strategic competitive advantage that included a quotation about the noted computer scientist, Alan Kay, with the catchphrase, "Perspective is worth 80 points of IQ."

This was the resulting presentation lead:

"In March 1975, a new office building was dedicated on Coyote Hill Road in Palo Alto, California. Now, ordinarily, I wouldn't much care about the dedication of an office building, and I can't imagine you would either. Except that this building was the new home to a still-youthful organization called the Palo Alto Research Center, better known as Xerox PARC—and you probably all owe your jobs to what was invented in that building.

"I know I certainly wouldn't be standing here before you if Bob Metcalfe and David Boggs hadn't joined forces there in the mid-70s to develop Ethernet technology.

"The creations that originated at Xerox PARC are mythic, and their creators are legendary. One of the most legendary of these is a man named Alan Kay, who is responsible for inventing object-oriented programming, the graphical user interface, and the very concept of a personal computer. Alan Kay has one of the most original minds in the technology field—perhaps one of the most original minds, period.

"But I come here, not to praise Alan Kay—nor to bury him—but to quote him. Alan Kay once said that perspective was worth 80 points of IQ. In other words, it's not how smart you are that matters, it's your ability to see things from different points of view. That's how innovation happens: by looking at things from a different angle and making connections that no one has made before."

After my client finished, the conference organizer met him backstage and told him that, unlike the previous day—when a more prominent CEO had some three hundred people leave his keynote before he finished because his approach was too "same-old, same-old"—not one person left before he finished.

So in your next presentation, look for a way to start that will take your audience by surprise (as long as you can make it relevant to your message). It may make you a little bit nervous—but then, the best communications solutions almost always do.

David Green is principal of UnCommon Knowledge (www.uncommon-knowledge. com), a corporate storytelling and strategic communications consultancy in the New York City area.

• • •

SHINING A LIGHT ON URBAN MYTHS OF PRESENTING
Jim Endicott

THERE ARE MANY "URBAN MYTHS" of the presentations world, or golden rules that, held up to the light of day, don't have quite the same amber hue they once possessed.

Here are four such time-honored tips and techniques that presenters might do well to reconsider in their planning and delivery.

1. Golden Rule: Use Five Bullet Points Per Slide

I find it pretty backwards when our dialog around being a better presenter devolves to discussions of number of bullets on a slide. First and foremost, the art of presenting is a relational skill, not a technical one. Granted, some people seem to need rules, but we miss the point.

Good presentations are not about bullets. Never have been. Never will be.

How about we talk about what types of visual content are remembered and why? Or how to structure meaningful messages that resonate with hearts and minds?

The Real Point

When using bullet points, most presenters will almost always read them. When given sub-bullets, presenters will read them as well. Bullets were a by-product of the original "outliners" that PowerPoint gave us eons ago to help form presentation messages.

Unfortunately, most presenters never learned that there's a big difference between *what* they need to say and *how* they need to say it (and show it).

Try this test. Give a presenter a bulleted slide to deliver on a topic that he is familiar with. He will undoubtedly turn to read it or deliver the content in a methodical bullet-by-bullet approach. *Now give him a single picture that covers the same topic and have him talk to it.* Something magical often happens. He spends a lot more time talking to his audience in a conversational manner!

There is a big lesson here. Did you get it? Bad PowerPoint can wreck otherwise good presenters.

2. Golden Rule: Audiences Expect You to Be Flawless

During my coaching workshops I often drag out a little buddy of mine, Mr. Wonderful. This little guy looks perfect with a winning smile and hair I wish I still had. And when you push his hand, he delivers a perfect message every time:

"No dear, you don't look at all fat in that dress. How could anything make you look fat!"

"Did you have a hard day, honey? Why don't you sit down and let me rub your feet."

"You're right. I don't know which way to go. I'll stop and ask directions."

After a handful of these gems, I ask the group how they would assess Mr. Wonderful's credibility? In perfect agreement, they tell me he has little or no credibility with them. Why? Because he's too perfect and polished.

If I somehow had it in my power as a presentation coach to transform anyone into the "perfect presenter," I would destroy his or her effectiveness. Our audiences are not looking for perfection. They are, however, looking for real people. Not TV reality show–type real but authentic, vulnerable, and honest communicators.

The Real Point

Be open. Be honest. Self-disclose things that allow your audience to know you better. Those types of presenters will be able to impact their audiences in ways the perfect presenter never could.

Our greatest position of influence will always be in coming *alongside* our audiences, not talking down to them or working overtime to establish our expertise. And the harder we try to be perfect the less that will be possible. (Prepared—yes. Perfect—no.)

3. Golden Rule: Tell 'Em What You're Going to Tell 'Em . . . Tell 'Em . . . Then Tell 'Em What You Told Them

Like many old axioms, there's a morsel of truth here, but it gets lost in the application. First, simple repetition (or repeated exposure to something) only means you run the real risk of upsetting audiences because you make them feel like children.

And secondly, just the habit of repeating something is no guarantee people will remember. Here's why.

Years ago researchers tested the whole idea of repetitive impressions on recall. I've repeated this fun little test in some of my coaching workshops. I bring two people up and put them in front of flip charts. Then I ask them to draw (in as much detail as possible) the front and back of a penny. They've obviously had tens of thousands of repeated exposures to those images. But true to the research, very few can even get close in their drawings. (Researchers called this "incidental exposure.")

Why? Because impressions (and ideas) must be relevant and meaningful to be remembered.

The Real Point

Repetition is only effective in recall if the message itself resonates with personal needs/issues. If the presenter's message is self-serving (as many are), then there is little chance anyone will care what you say no matter how many times you may say it.

Even worse, put that point in the form of bullets or raw data and recall will be even more adversely impacted. That's because intellectual material is processed on the left side of the brain, which generally only supports short-term memory.

4. Golden Rule: Better Presentation Software Will Make Me a Better Presenter

In the general presentations community there's been a recurring push for "serious" presenters (and designers) to move to more "leading edge" and trendy presentation software tools. Everyone is looking for an edge—and I get that. But I have a question: Why is it I can see really bad presentations produced in tools like Keynote or Prezi and yet, to this day, see beautiful and effective visual communication tools come out of PowerPoint 2000—a thirteen-year-old software product?

The answer is (and always will be) this important truth: Talented and creative people will make works of communication art no matter what canvas they're using. And the vast majority of everyone else will continue to look for the next trendy tool to give them an edge, but you'll always be able to tell the difference. Form never trumps substance.

The Real Point

No one will ever be able to make a common-sense wizard. Don't get me wrong. There's nothing wrong with some of the latest presentation software packages. But I learned a long time ago a very painful (and expensive) reality: I can buy high-end Nike golf balls and still not hit them like pro golfer Phil Mickelson does. And the only ones who seem to benefit from my purchase are the folks in the golf pro shop.

Jim Endicott is the president of Distinction Communication Inc. (www.distinction-services.com), a Newberg, Oregon, consulting firm specializing in message development, presentation design, and delivery skills coaching.

• • •

THREE STEPS TO HELP YOUR DATA STAND OUT AND BE REMEMBERED
Mike Parkinson

HOW DO YOU USE data to prove that you have the best idea or solution to an audience's problem?

Your presentation states over and over that your solution saves money. But what does that mean to your audience? A dollar a month? A thousand dollars a day? Is it significant enough for them to invest in your solution and change their current entrenched process?

They want and expect you to prove your claim, so what is the best way to do that?

Step 1: Provide Real-World Data

One of the simplest ways to sway your audience is to back up your assertions with real numbers. To show how your solution saves money, you could provide formulas or tables that compare your solution's costs to the current solution based on research conducted by a reputable resource.

Unfortunately, this approach can be difficult to digest and is far from memorable and compelling. Look at the example in Table 1.1. Is this the fastest way to analyze data?

Table 1.1.   Lumber Shipments by Region

	Jan	Feb	Mar	Apr	May	June	July	Aug	Sept	Oct	Nov	Dec
Region 1	17	26	53	41	36	45	23	42	29	35	31	37
Region 2	55	43	97	78	62	89	67	54	47	61	65	77

Because, like you, viewers are often resource starved, rushed, and hate reading through mountains of data, it is in our best interest to make data analysis as easy as possible.

Although a well-researched spreadsheet of your solution is a perfect first step to support your claim, we need to turn this data into something your audience can quickly digest and remember.

Step 2: Turn Data into a Compelling Quantitative Chart

Consolidate data into bite-size chunks that can be analyzed quickly. (You can include your spreadsheets as back-up data when applicable.)

Quantitative charts—like bar charts, area charts, line charts, and pie charts—make it easy to compare data.

Many software packages allow you to generate charts from your data or make your own charts, helping you better visualize the comparisons between the solutions.

How easy is it to compare the numbers in Figure 1.1?

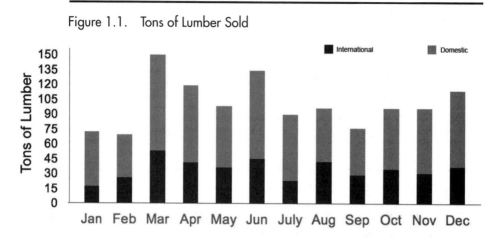

Figure 1.1. Tons of Lumber Sold

Although much improved over a table, a quantitative chart alone is not that memorable. Let's face it. You've seen countless bar charts, area charts, line charts, and pie charts every year. What makes this bar chart stand out from all the others you've seen? It looks like a generic chart rendered in Excel. Would you remember this chart a day, a week, a year from now? If you are like most people, probably not.

Step 3: Use Visual Embellishment

The Department of Computer Science at the University of Saskatchewan in Canada conducted an experiment to determine whether visual embellishment in information charts was a detractor. Here's a quote from an excerpt in the study:

> "Guidelines for designing information charts often state that the presentation should reduce 'chart junk'—visual embellishments that are not essential to understanding the data. In contrast, some popular chart designers wrap the presented data in detailed and elaborate imagery, raising the questions of whether this imagery is really as detrimental to understanding as has been proposed, and whether the visual embellishment may have other benefits.
>
> "To investigate these issues, we conducted an experiment that compared embellished charts with plain ones, and

measured both interpretation accuracy and long-term recall. *We found that people's accuracy in describing the embellished charts was no worse than for plain charts, and that their recall after a two-to-three-week gap was significantly better."*

Figure 1.2, published in the study's findings, shows a chart (on the left) developed by Nigel Holmes, a renowned visual communicator, and a "plain version" next to it.

Which drew your attention first? Which is more memorable?

Figure 1.2. Comparison of Charts

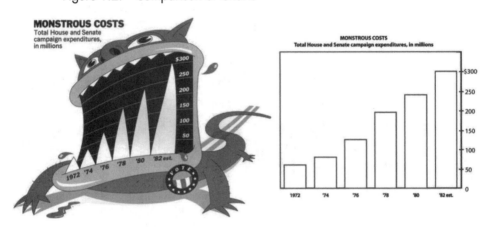

In an interesting twist, Holmes designed his chart as a personification of the "monstrous" costs. (See whether you remember his chart in a few days. I'm betting that you will.)

We don't always have the creative license to transform our data into something as fun as the "monstrous" chart, but we can learn that quantitative charts don't always need to follow the plain chart mold to communicate our data.

In fact, thinking outside the standard quantitative chart by using a visual metaphor, simile, analogy, or icon/symbol will grab your audience's attention and help increase their recollection of your data.

So what kind of embellishment can we use on our original chart to make our "saves money" assertion really stand out? We could

replace the bars with stacks of money, showing money literally pil-
ing up from the savings realized from using our solution. We could
add callout text that reads "38 percent cost savings."

Depending on your solution, you can weave your product
(or something associated with your product or solution) into the
chart. For example, Figure 1.3 is a chart for a lumber company
depicting shipments made throughout the year. I used different
wood stains to show the difference in international versus domes-
tic shipments.

Figure 1.3.   Annual Lumber Shipments

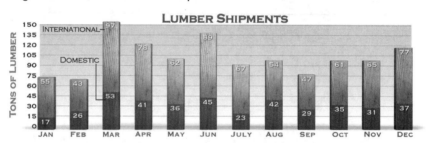

Most quantitative charts are far from unique and, therefore, fail
to stand out. Using a visually embellished quantitative chart helps
ensure your data impresses your audience, is remembered, and ultimately, helps you succeed.

Bottom line: Challenge yourself to think beyond the standard
charts and create something truly memorable. It will leave a far
more lasting impression on your audience.

Mike Parkinson, the founder and CEO of Billion Dollar Graphics (www.billion-
dollargraphics.com) in Annandale, Virginia, is a graphic design consultant, visual
communication expert, and multi-published author.

•   •   •

SEVEN TIPS FOR POWERFUL SIT-DOWN PRESENTATIONS
Dianna Booher

WHETHER IT'S ANSWERING AN off-handed query, "How's the project going?" or selling your ideas for conducting a new employee survey, every presentation you make is an opportunity to establish an executive presence and move up in your organization.

Consider these tips for improving both the substance and style of your next presentation so that you can speak up with confidence and authority.

1. Don't "Let Down" for Sit-Down Presentations

In a business setting, you may make presentations to only a few people seated around a conference table or desk. Although there is no correlation between audience size and importance of the outcome, consider several issues in light of the informal setting.

First, consider the group's expectations. Do not assume that because the audience is small, its members do not expect a formal presentation—visuals and the works.

Second, because you are seated around a desk or table—at eye level with the group—you must convey your enthusiasm, assertiveness, and authority at "half mast" through your facial expressions, posture, and voice.

Sitting down may tempt you to slouch, but don't. Sit comfortably erect, leaning slightly forward in your chair to show attentiveness and enthusiasm for your subject. Sit back in your chair to convey openness to questions.

Position yourself to maintain eye contact with everyone in the room. Do not get stuck between two listeners so that you have to turn your head back and forth with each point, as though you are watching a game of table tennis. If possible, remove any physical obstacles that block vision or create "distance" between you and your audience.

Sitting down or standing up—decisions count either way.

2. Make Statistics Experiential

People digest numbers with great difficulty. Graphs and charts help. But if you can go beyond these common visuals, do so. For example, one manager speaking before his peers at IBM about his budget being cut dramatically yanked off his jacket to reveal his white shirt—with great big holes cut out of the sides and back. Amid the laughter, he made his point dramatically and memorably.

To demonstrate the cost of absenteeism to your organization, have your group complete a worksheet on "Employee Ed" who misses six days a month three times a year. Then increase those absences per warehouse in each division as the audience calculates on their worksheets. The numbers will come alive as they themselves work with the changing results.

3. Never Let Facts Speak for Themselves

Facts need interpretation. According to Mark Twain, "There are three kinds of lies: lies, damned lies, and statistics." If you don't believe this, tune in to the next political campaign. People can make facts and numbers mean almost anything. Interpret yours so that your listeners draw the same conclusions you intend.

4. Use Analogies to Provide a Consistent Framework

Think how many times you have heard the functioning of the human eye and its parts compared to the working of a camera—an excellent analogy for clarifying a complex process. Or how often have you heard complex routers referred to as a telephone switchboard—with each part of the equipment explained as it compares to a small telephone system?

Probably the best-known analogies and allegories are Biblical parables and Aesop's fables. "Concern over the unrepentant means leaving the ninety-nine sheep to look for the lost one." "The tortoise runs a slow but steady pace and crosses the finish line a winner."

Such visual or emotional analogies help audiences follow a lengthy presentation step by step.

5. Remember That Timing Indicates Emphasis

In general, a good rule of thumb for allocation of your overall time is to spend 10 to 15 percent of your time on the opening, 70 to 85 percent on the body, and 5 to 10 percent on the closing. This allows slightly more time up-front in the introduction to grab attention, "win over" a hostile or uninterested group, and establish credibility than to close the presentation.

If your presentation includes an involved action plan, that section most likely should be part of the body of your presentation, and your close should focus on the final persuasive push toward the decision to act.

On the other hand, you may discover that you need to cut. In doing so, always keep the audience's preferences in mind. Think of your presentation as a roadmap. If your audience wants to take only interstate highways to their destination, do not pencil in all the farm-to-market roads along the way. This merely clutters the map.

With regard to information overload, as John Brockmann so aptly put it, "Most houseplants in the U.S. are killed by over-watering."

6. Use Metaphors, Similes, and Other Analogies to Clarify and Aid Retention

A metaphor is a word or phrase substituted for another to suggest similarity. For example: "My friend is my Rock of Gibraltar," "Time is money," "Kill that idea," "That question will be the litmus test," "This new product line will be our insurance policy against obsolescence."

A simile compares two things with the actual words *like* or *as* in the analogy. Recently, I've heard business presenters use examples such as these: "Trying to process these data with your computers is like trying to mow your lawn with a pair of scissors"; "Your files are like athletic socks and dress socks; you don't need both every day. Access should determine how you should store them"; "This new legislation before Congress is like throwing a nuclear bomb at an ant hill—and missing the ant hill."

The more complex the idea, the more important it is to simplify and illustrate by comparison.

7. Never Ramble on Past the Point of High Impact

Anything you say after your polished point of close dilutes your impact. Do not ramble on with anticlimactic drivel. Say it and stop.

Dianna Booher is the CEO of Booher Consultants (www.booher.com) and works with organizations to increase their productivity and effectiveness through better oral, written, interpersonal, and cross-functional communication.

• • •

SIX BIG DON'TS FOR ENDING YOUR PRESENTATION
Ben Decker

EVEN THE STRONGEST SPEAKERS can undercut a whole presentation with three seconds of wobbly indecision at the end. Those few seconds amount to the last impression you leave with your audience—it's the last picture people will remember of you. You've spent your whole presentation building credibility for yourself and your idea, and that last impression has everything to do with how you hold yourself.

Watch your nonverbal behavior and body language. Not even a line like Patrick Henry's, "Give me liberty. . .!" can bail you out if you act nervous, disgusted, insincere, or hurried. Here are six essential don'ts for ending your presentation.

1. Never Blackball Yourself

. . . with a critical grimace, a shake of the head, eyes rolled upward, a disgusted little sigh. So what if you're displeased with yourself? Don't insult your audience by letting them know you were awful; they probably thought you were pretty good.

One lip curl in those last three seconds can wreck thirty minutes of credibility-building. Keep a light smile on your face, and you can grimace at the mirror in the bathroom later if you want.

2. Don't Step Backwards

If anything, take a half-step toward your listeners at the end. Stepping back is a physical retreat, and audiences subconsciously pick up on this cue. While you're at it, don't step back verbally either. Softening your voice and trailing off toward the end obviously doesn't sound confident. Maintain your strong vocal projection, annunciation, and pitch variety. You need to end with a bang, not a whimper.

3. Don't Look Away

Some speakers harken back to the last visual aid or PowerPoint slide, as if for reinforcement. Some people look aside, unwilling to confront listeners dead in the eye at the last words. Murmuring "thank you" while staring off somewhere else isn't the last impression you want to leave. Maintain good eye communication throughout.

4. Don't Leave Your Hands in a Gestured Position

In our programs we recommend using the resting ready position (arms gently at the sides) at the end to physically signal your audience you're finished. You must let them go visually, in addition to the closing remarks you're making. If you keep your hands up at waist level, you look as if you have something more to say. In speaking, think of yourself as the gracious host or hostess as you drop your hands with an appreciative thank you.

5. Don't Rush to Collect Your Papers

Or visual aids or displays. Stop and chat with people if the meeting is breaking up, then begin to tidy up in a calm, unhurried manner. Otherwise, you may contradict your calm, confident demeanor as a presenter. Behavioral cues are being picked up by your audience throughout the entire presentation experience, even during post-presentation.

If you sit down and grimace or huff and puff, listeners notice that, too.

6. Don't Move on the Last Word

Plant your feet and hold still for a half-beat after the *you* in thank you. Think about adding some lightness and smile with your thank you to show your comfort and ease. You don't want to look anxious to get out of there. If anything, you want to let people know you've enjoyed being with them and are sorry you have to go. Don't rush off.

Paying attention to your behaviors at the end of your presentation, whether formal at the lectern or informal standing at a meeting, will project the confidence and credibility you seek.

Ben Decker is the president of Decker Communications (www.decker.com), a presentation skills consulting firm that coaches senior executives and managers to transform business communications.

• • •

2

What's in It for Them?

DEVELOPING AUDIENCE-CENTRIC MESSAGES

Chances are you've experienced this pain. You're listening to a presenter who's spent little time considering the audience's point of view, or those issues that had you enthused about attending the presentation—given it's promising title—in the first place. The presenter has just dragged you through forty minutes of material that only touches on five minutes' worth of your relevant need.

Or perhaps the speaker has done little to customize a cookie-cutter presentation he's given countless times before. While he does a good job of highlighting features of his company's products or services, you see no connection between his slides and your areas of immediate need. The interaction becomes like two ships passing in the night.

Presentations conceived and delivering from the audience's eyes, that provide information carefully chosen to help listeners begin addressing their most pressing business challenges *tomorrow*, quickly move from mediocre to memorable in the audience's mind. Master presenters understand that requires running all of their slides, data, or narrative through the "What's in it for me?" filter through which every audience member evaluates a presentation.

• • •

THE DELICATE ART OF PRESENTING TO THE CEO

Sue Hershkowitz-Coore

THE CEO AGREED to see me for fifteen minutes. I've had good-byes that last longer than that, but I was still thrilled. I was getting a one-to-one. But what could I say (in fifteen minutes, no less) that would not only create a great impression but would persuade him to want to further engage my services?

What Not to Do

I worked on a slide deck showing what we had accomplished with the CEO's team so far. I don't use bullets in my deck so I created a flourish of fabulous photos to demonstrate his company's success. It was a strong deck, and if I had been making a one-hour presentation to a group of department heads—and I were using the fifteen-minute deck to kick off the discussion—it would have been perfect.

But I wasn't talking to managers; I was talking to "the man" and I guessed that he didn't want to see my fancy photos or even be talked to.

Scratch the deck.

What to Do

I decided that the only thing that was important to him was future success. Instead of regaling him with what we had accomplished (truly, if he hadn't thought I had value, he wouldn't be seeing me—the same is true for you). I tucked my computer away, prepared to talk about any of the past details but more determined just to hear what he had to say and what vision he had for me.

There were two other things that I considered before walking in:

1. The CEO is no different from anyone else who holds a job. He or she is fearful. CEOs are fearful of the same things that I'm frightened of (except maybe much more so). They don't want to:

    a. Fail, personally or organizationally

    b. Be embarrassed (see above)

    c. Make bad choices (above again)

2. The CEO wants what every salesperson wants. They look for ways to:

    a. Sell more, more easily, at a better margin

    b. Make customers happy, happier, happiest

    c. Beat out the competition in everything, including the competition's existing customers

I walked in, thanked him for his time, and spoke my truth: I have a slide deck prepared to show you what we've accomplished. But with the fifteen minutes that we have together, it may be a more valuable use of your time if I can learn from you. Where would you like to go with this initiative?

Then I shut up.

And for the next twelve minutes, he talked about ideas to *grow* the project.

I recapped, thanked him for his time, and told him he could count on me to work with his team to get it done.

Sell Better by Selling Less

If you are trying to persuade your own C-level to buy into an idea, it's important to make sure you're fully prepared. But also consider doing these things:

*   State your purpose and your project goal (be specific), and ask how that relates to the future she or he envisions for the company.

- Then speak your truth, the question you are truly wondering about. Ask: Does this align with your plans to take this company into the next decade? Is this goal the right priority? Am I headed in the right direction? Would it be helpful if I provided background on my thinking?

- Also ask what would be the best approach. "May I ask your initial thoughts or would you prefer to see a few minutes of the deck I've prepared?"

- Be quick! Create any slide deck to help solidify the ideas in your mind, *not* to expand them. Someone once said that if your idea doesn't fit on the back of your business card, you don't have an idea.

- Spend as much time thinking about the questions you'll ask as you do on creating the perfect PowerPoint deck.

People, including C-levels, usually tell us everything we need to know if we just ask.

Sue Hershkowitz-Coore (www.speakersue.com) is a corporate consultant, communications specialist, and internationally recognized professional speaker.

• • •

ARE YOUR KEY TAKEAWAYS A NEEDLE IN A HAYSTACK?
Jim Endicott

IMAGINE FOR A MOMENT I hid a set of keys for a new Lexus in one of those personal storage lockers at Portland International Airport. And all you had to do is find the specific door, put in the key, and it's all yours!

My job? I just had to explain how to get there through the busy and hyper-distracting environment of an international airport. It's not that I want to make it hard for you to find. To the contrary— I really want you to find it. But we may have a challenge. I like to use words to explain things. Lots of them.

If I show you a map . . . you get it. But if I give you a turn-by-turn (bullet-by-bullet) set of instructions . . . well, your Lexus may be waiting for a while in the parking lot.

This metaphoric dilemma is what presentation audiences experience every day of the week. If they didn't know better, they just might suspect you were working overtime to make sure there was no way they could possibly "get" the really important stuff you intended for them.

The problem? You've been ruminating with your presentations message for days, maybe weeks. They have mere minutes to understand your intent. You labored over your presentation slides for hours . . . they have thirty seconds to figure one out.

We've come a long way in being able to develop good presentations, yet in some ways have not progressed very far at all. Despite our enhanced ability to fade, pan, zoom, create motion, append media, present online, present offline, and choose from an ever-growing array of design layouts and shape effects, we've lost track of our prime directive.

(Seek to "do no harm" comes to mind, but perhaps there's something even more important.)

At the end of the time you've been given . . . after all the collective hours of invested effort and energy . . . and at the conclusion of precious time invested by your audience to disengage from other priorities and be present . . . *they must remember.*

And this is where we too often let them down. We think software features = recall. They don't. We believe graphical embellishments by themselves create message clarity. They cannot. And like someone who has relied on a cane long after the pain subsided, it has become an unfortunate part of who we are and what we do.

The process has somehow become more important than the outcome and we've abrogated a job that is ours and ours alone: creating message clarity and simplicity so others can truly understand.

So consider this personal challenge:

What if your personal compensation for the entire month was dependent on one single thing?

Here it is. If those sitting on the receiving end of your next presentation could remember and repeat back a simple few points they believed you wanted to get across, you were paid. If they could not or struggled to somehow distill those things out of the forty or fifty points of emphasis you made during your presentation, your check went into a drawer until they could.

What would your next presentation look like?

I'm guessing your visuals would be amazingly simple. And those dozens of points you previously wanted to communicate? They would likely refine themselves down to a few simple ideas illustrated in visually rich ways. Those key messages might also be underscored with personal stories to make them powerfully relevant.

And the presentation closing? A single word or two on screen, reinforced and related to their lives.

Desiring to communicate so much, we often end up giving audiences nothing at all.

So I will leave you with a few simple things:

Set Clear Expectations on Slide 1 and Deliver on Your Promise

Where are you taking them and what's the prize at the end of the journey?

Make the Path Simple and Straight

Create a simple closing slide first that becomes the litmus test for all you say and be clear how the journey relates to that prize. (Fifty-slide presentations are easy to create. Ten-slide presentations are the mark of a great communicator.)

Let Your Audience Know When They've Arrived

Many presentations seem to end simply because the presenter ran out of slides. In the simplest of terms and in the briefest amount of time, conclude your presentation by serving people up on a platter what you want them to remember and why. Simple. Crisp. Straightforward.

OK, so I don't really have a Lexus waiting for you at the Portland airport and there is no locker with a key. But the point is hopefully crystal-clear. Don't make it hard for your audience to walk away with something important. Clear away the visual and messaging obstacles to real understanding.

And most of all: Remember why you're there in the first place.

Jim Endicott is president of Distinction Communication Inc. (www.distinction-services.com), a Newberg, Oregon, consulting firm specializing in message development, presentation design, and delivery skills coaching.

• • •

SHIFT FOCUS FROM YOUR DATA TO YOUR AUDIENCE
Dave Paradi

A FEW MONTHS AGO I was advising a senior executive at a research firm on an upcoming presentation. This executive was about to present data to a client, and the desire was that the client understand what that data meant to its business.

As we chatted, the dominant issue became clear. She was focused on the data, where it came from, how it had been collected, and proving that the numbers were accurate. All important aspects to her, *but not important to the audience.* The audience didn't care as much about the origins of the data as it did about what that data meant to improving its business.

They cared about what directions the data suggested, what the data implied for future initiatives, and what they should do now given the results of the research.

Once she heard what I was saying, she was able to view her presentation from a totally different perspective—*she stepped into the shoes of her audience.* She refocused her presentation on the key conclusions from the research and gave a few points of proof from the data. It helped the audience understand and act on what she presented.

She also mentioned that she found it easier to present because she was focused on the few key messages and could stay on track without getting lost in the details of the data.

Switching Focus

The key for this executive, and for many presenters, is to switch the focus from the *data* to the *audience.* By taking the audience's perspective, you gain great clarity on what they're looking for and what is important to them.

If you have a lot of data, you'll see that the audience is only interested in the conclusions, not the data itself. They don't need to hear all the background behind the statistics. They need to know what they should do based on what the data and analysis have shown.

Make this switch in your perspective, and you will find your data-driven presentations become far more effective and memorable.

Dave Paradi runs the Think Outside the Slide website (www.thinkoutsidetheslide .com), is a consultant on high-stakes presentations, author of seven books, and a Microsoft PowerPoint Most Valuable Professional (MVP).

•   •   •

USE MENUS TO CREATE AUDIENCE-CENTERED PRESENTATIONS
Ellen Finkelstein

IS YOUR AUDIENCE important to you? You bet. If you want to win them over, you need to consider their needs over yours. Most presenters force-feed the audience a predetermined message. This linear type of presentation gives viewers no choice about what they see.

For a large audience, this is usually expected, but in a small setting, such as when you're trying to sell a product or service or recommend a strategy, your audience members are powerful people who may have strong opinions about what they want to hear.

I'm going to show you how to create a non-linear presentation—using a menu—that lets your audience have control over the direction of your content. This technique also gives you the flexibility to change the direction of your presentation at a moment's notice, depending on the situation.

Because of websites, people are accustomed to choosing what they see from a vast amount of hierarchically arranged information. A website gives people control. They click the link that interests them and go where they want. If viewers find what they want quickly and easily, they're happy.

In terms of a presentation, your audience may be stuck in the room, but their attentiveness can easily go out the window.

The advantages of a non-linear presentation are

- You put your audience first by allowing them to choose the direction of the presentation.

- You can make last-minute changes based on the time available and feedback from the audience.

- You can include additional, optional information that you may or may not deliver.

Think of Your Presentation as a Website

To create a non-linear, menu-based presentation, you organize it hierarchically. You create a presentation that functions like a website.

Start with a title page—in web jargon this is called a splash page. This is nothing other than your usual title slide.

Then add a second slide that will function as a home page. Add a title, a brief explanation of what you are offering your audience, and a menu. The title and explanation are an overview of the content of the presentation, just as the home page of a website quickly lets you know the purpose and value of the site.

Make this content short, but enticing, so that the audience feels that they'll obtain useful, valuable information. If you have a catchphrase that describes what you're about, you can use that.

Create a Menu

How do you create the menu? You'll achieve the best-looking results using AutoShapes or Action Buttons, both available from the Drawing toolbar in PowerPoint. Action Buttons are nice because they look like web buttons. Use the blank Action Button and enter the text you need.

Keep the text short, as on a website button. Resize and format your buttons as you want.

Note: When you choose an Action Button, the Action Settings dialog box opens. You can use it to create hyperlinks, but since you're not ready to do that yet, just click Cancel.

Your menu can be utilitarian or extravagant, depending on your topic, audience, and presenting style. Figure 2.1 on the next page shows a utilitarian example for a human resources department.

Figure 2.2 is an example for the sales representative of a hotel. This example uses callouts and is much more sales-oriented. But the concept is the same.

Figure 2.1.   Chart for an HR Department

Figure 2.2.   Image for a Presentation

Your creativity is only limited by your imagination. For example, you can insert pictures and add hyperlinks to them. You can add a hyperlink to any object on your slide. The only caution is against adding hyperlinks to text. When you do so, PowerPoint underlines the text and applies the Hyperlink color from your color scheme. This may not be the best solution for two reasons:

- The underlined text can be hard to read and doesn't look very good.

- Most people pay no attention to the Hyperlink color, and it may not contrast well with your background. Furthermore, when a link is used, it takes on the Followed Hyperlink color, which may also not be legible.

Create Sections Organized by Topic

At the end of the process, you'll turn each menu item into a hyperlink. But first, you need to create the content slides. For each menu topic, create the slides that contain the content that you want to present.

The first slide of each topic should have the same title as the menu item. As on a website, this helps everyone know they've arrived in the right place. In the human resources example, this means that clicking on the Medical Coverage button leads to a slide like the one in Figure 2.3.

Figure 2.3.   Medical Coverage Slide

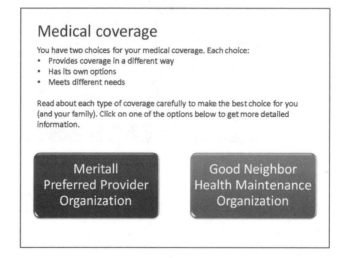

You should end up with a section for each menu item.

You can also create subsections to create a more hierarchical structure. The Medical Coverage page has two buttons with links to two subsections, one on each type of medical coverage. However, don't make the structure too complex, because you need to be able to navigate easily.

Add Hyperlinks on the Menu

To add the hyperlinks, select a menu item. If you used an AutoShape or Action Button, be sure to click on the edge to select it, rather than on the text. If you click on the text, PowerPoint adds the hyperlink to the text, not the button. Aside from the issues I raised previously, when you hyperlink the text, you need to click exactly on the text to use the hyperlink. It's easier if you can just click anywhere on the shape or button.

To create the hyperlink (Figure 2.4), follow these steps:

1. Press Ctrl + K or choose Insert > Hyperlink. (In PowerPoint 2007, choose Insert tab > Links group > Hyperlink.)

Figure 2.4.   Creating Hyperlinks

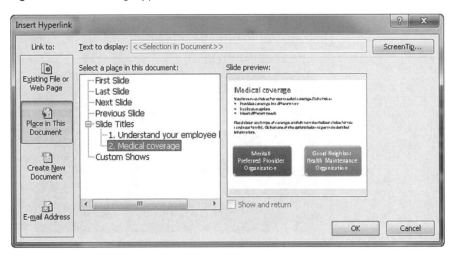

2. In the Hyperlink dialog box, click the Place in This Document button on the left and you'll see a list of the slides in the current presentation.

3. Choose the slide that you want to hyperlink to.

4. Click OK.

Do this for each menu item. If you created subsections, add hyperlinks to the buttons that should link to those sections.

Add Hyperlinks Back to the Main Menu

When you click a hyperlink in Slide Show view, you'll immediately go to the proper slide. Then you'll continue from slide to slide until you finish that topic.

Tip 1: If you don't realize that you're at the end of a topic section, you'll continue to the next section. Oops! Put a graphic on the last slide of each section to remind you. An unobtrusive line or triangle on a corner is enough. On this slide, the horizontal line at the bottom indicates the end of a section, as shown in Figure 2.5.

Figure 2.5.   End of Section Slide

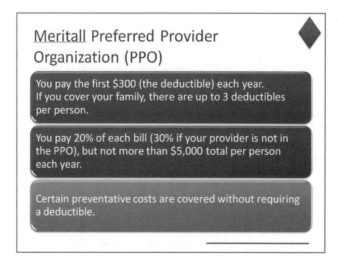

But how do you get back to the menu? You need to create links on each of the slides to return to the menu (or sub-menu, if any), just as on a website. To create a button to the main menu, you can use the Home Action button, which is a familiar icon in your browser. Be sure to hyperlink it to your menu slide, which may not be your first slide. Otherwise, you can use any object and link it to the menu. The diamond at the upper-right corner of the above slide is the link back to the menu.

Tip 2: Add the hyperlink to one object, and then copy it to the rest of the slides. The hyperlink will come along with the copy, so you won't have to add the hyperlink on each slide.

Tip 3: Create an invisible button. The link back to the menu doesn't have to be visible, and clicking on it makes the transition seem magical! Place an AutoShape in one of the corners of the slide where you can easily find it. To make an invisible button, right-click the selected AutoShape and choose Format AutoShape. On the Colors and Lines tab, set the Line Color drop-down list to No Line. Then drag the Transparency slider in the Fill section to 99 percent.

For a broader range of resources, you can create links to other presentations or files, or to anywhere on the Internet, by choosing the Existing File or Web Page button on the left side of the Hyperlink dialog box. Just be sure you have those files with you, or an Internet connection, if you travel to give your presentation.

Delivering Your Menu-Based Presentation

When you give your presentation, you can then present your home page and explain the information available using the menu. If a member of the audience indicates an interest, go that way.

If not, you can use the links to direct the presentation yourself. You might ask the audience: "What would you like to hear about first?" In this way, you deliver a presentation that is truly audience-centered. You know that you are providing the information they want to hear. Moreover, you immediately involve the audience. The result will be greater success for your presentations.

Why not just present your company's website? There are several reasons:

- The website probably doesn't contain all the specialized information you want to present and probably contains lots of information your audience doesn't need.

- Getting a fast, reliable Internet connection is tricky. You don't want prospects to have to wait for pages to download (or worse, not download at all).

- Websites limit graphics and colors for downloading speed and consistency over various platforms and browsers. In PowerPoint, you can create the compelling look you want.

Try Something New

Before giving your first non-linear, menu-based presentation, try it out on a friendly audience, perhaps some colleagues. Practice using the navigation. Web-based presentations take some getting used to for both the presenter and the audience, but you'll soon find that they offer incredible flexibility and power.

Ellen Finkelstein (www.ellenfinkelstein.com) is a noted presentation skills consultant and trainer, a PowerPoint Most Valuable Professional (MVP), and a multi-published author in the presentations field.

• • •

HOW TO USE ANALOGIES IN PRESENTATIONS
Scott Schwertly

I F USED CORRECTLY, analogies can greatly strengthen and nuance a presentation. Like most vague literary terms that we haven't thought twice about since high school, it's helpful to start with a definition: An analogy is a comparison between two things, typically on the basis of their structure and for the purpose of explanation or clarification. It's essentially a complex metaphor, and it's certainly one of the best ways to clarify dense, difficult information for your audience.

Here are some tips on how to use analogies effectively in presentations.

Statistics Don't Stick

We've discussed at length ways to effectively use statistics. None of those methods involve simply stating a statistic and moving on. Statistics don't stick with audiences; people don't remember cumbersome data if it's not presented in a framework that provides meaning for them. Chip and Dan Heath reinforce this in their book *Made to Stick*, writing, "Statistics will, and should, almost always be used to illustrate a *relationship*. It's more important for people to remember the relationship than the number."

Using appropriate analogies is an effective way to establish that relationship. The *Made to Stick* authors cite the Beyond War movement in the 1980s as an example of using a compelling analogy to provide context for an abstract idea.

The group was on a mission to prove to people the real danger of nuclear weapons, and they needed to make this abstract, vague notion a tangible one. They did this at various "house parties" by dropping BBs into a metal bucket. The representative dropped one BB in the bucket to represent the Hiroshima bomb, and then spoke to the calamitous effects of that event.

Then he dropped ten BBs in the bucket, representing the power of the missiles on one nuclear submarine. Last, he dropped five thousand BBs in the bucket, one for every nuclear warhead in the world.

This analogy provided a poignant framework for the audience. They would remember for a long time the haunting sound of the

BBs hitting the metal, and that sound would be forever tied to the impact of a nuclear weapon.

Vague, abstract information doesn't stick with audiences. Tangible, visual analogies do.

Scale and Topic Matters

One of the most important considerations when dealing with analogy is scale. It's imperative to choose the right scale, which means selecting the most tangible one possible. We've all heard analogies with a scale "reaching from the earth to the moon X amount of times." That can be an appropriate scale if you're dealing with a very large statistic, but if you're talking about a few miles, that scale would be much too large.

Choose a framework for your analogy that imparts a compelling impression on the audience. They should come away from your analogy with an "Aha!" or "Wow!" reaction because the comparison feels so tangible.

And be sure to choose an appropriate analogy in terms of topic. If you're speaking to Europeans, soccer might be a great analogy to invoke when talking about percentages. But if you're speaking to Americans, perhaps football would be better. Make the analogy easy for the audience to relate to as well as understand. Don't forget that your audience's needs are the most important thing. Fashion your analogies accordingly.

Use Wisely

Regardless of all the benefits of using analogies, proceed with caution when crafting a presentation with one. *Remember that your audience doesn't know what you know as well as you do, so keep everything as simple as possible.* It's easy to mislead or confuse people with a convoluted analogy, so put yourself in the audience's shoes before you decide whether it works or not.

The whole point of using an analogy is to make things easier to understand, not more difficult, so use them only when you're dealing with recondite material. Don't make something more complicated than it needs to be.

And last, and perhaps most importantly, beware of bringing analogies full circle or referring to them at several different times during your presentation. The meaning can easily become confused, and you can lose the audience by inducing a "Wait, what is he talking about?" moment.

Use analogies wisely, and only when they will, without a doubt, help your audience more fully understand your presentation.

Scott Schwertly is the CEO and founder of Ethos 3 (www.ethos3.com), a leading presentation design and training company.

• • •

LEADERSHIP COMMUNICATION ASKS MORE OF US
Jim Endicott

A FEW YEARS BACK we received a call from a large, internationally known manufacturing company. Here's how it went. "Hi, Jim, we'd need your company to come in and consult with us about some communication issues a few of our senior managers are having." We came prepared to discuss our presentation skills workshops.

But the issue at hand was something altogether different.

As we soon discovered, the senior managers in question had worked their way up through the company for twenty years but were now struggling. The responsibility of leadership was now asking of them something they had never learned in engineering school.

Over the course of their careers, most had made an art form out of their ability to populate PowerPoint charts, graphs, and table slides. But when faced with the need to motivate, challenge, and align those they were leading, their tool kits were empty. You might as well have asked them to ballroom dance.

Sadly, this scenario plays out more than you might think today. Talented and capable managers often struggle with navigating the transition from valued mid-level manager to senior leader in an effective way.

The Truth About the Facts

You don't need to look any further than the hundreds of charting options in PowerPoint or the five levels of sub-bullet defaults in the Master Slide to understand that the tool was built for the conveyance of raw information.

And as intriguing as the idea may be to take a whack at creating a radar, pyramid, or donut chart, most of us come to our senses and ask the all-important question . . . *Why?*

The truth is it's simply quicker and easier to pour our information into a preexisting mold that may or may not be easier for our audiences to actually "get." Too many leaders today have made facts and data their sole channel for communicating with those they lead and it has impaired not only their personal effectiveness but also their ability to create bottom-line results.

We may help people better understand some key business metrics and accomplish some level of understanding, but obtaining an employee's or peer's agreement, personal ownership, and motivation to take action may be something else altogether. Therein lies the challenge.

Information that's presented to others in the form of charts, data, bullets, or some other intellectualized communication material is making its appeal to the left side of the brain. That part of the brain is uniquely designed to process material that is logical, orderly, and methodical.

OK, so what's the problem? Appealing to the left side of the brain has some major limitations for leaders who aspire to be more than just purveyors of data and information.

Consider these three points:

Raw data is rarely memorable. Think of that college final examination when you crammed all night long before the big test. How much of that information did you retain a week or a month later? Can you recall the bulleted information from several slides you saw in a presentation just last week? The answer is typically no.

Unless it impacts our paychecks (a message that has pronounced right-brain emotional appeal!), the information is not encoded in a way that is meaningful and retrievable. Think of memory as a long path through the woods and recall the mechanism we use to help others find their way back to an important thought or idea.

Remember, raw data = no bread crumbs.

Defense-intensive. If we use intellectualized material as our sole leadership communication vehicle, we must be prepared for the often cerebral, more defense-intensive response it evokes. There's certainly a time to debate and challenge business metrics. We absolutely need them to measure, analyze, and chart relevant courses, but we can expect others to respond intellectually. "What's the source of your data?" "Is that current information?" "Your goals are not realistic for my team!"

Low persuasive value. Think about this question: The last time you were motivated by information, was it because of the statistic itself or because of an understanding of the personal impact it represented?

You may be able to get your direct reports to respond robotically to the latest quarterly business goals or out of fear for missing a performance bonus, but not often enough out of a deeply embraced and shared organizational goal or vision—the kind that drives extraordinary performance and personal sacrifice over the long haul.

Taking Messages to a Deeper Level

There's a lot being written these days about effective leadership. And the interaction we have with a Portland-area executive MBA program would seem to validate that today's managers are much better equipped for analyzing business metrics and dissecting profit and loss statements.

But if facts aren't an effective mechanism for winning the hearts and minds of busy employees, peers, or customers—what is?

The answer is found in the feedback we receive hundreds of times a year when we ask this question to those attending our workshops: "Who were your most inspiring and motivating leaders and why?"

In all the years we've asked that question, not once has someone touted a leader's ability to create killer 3D bar charts. And we've never heard about the amazing way they present Excel spreadsheets. Here's what we do hear, however:

- "They used *personal stories* to help create a relevant context for what we were up against."

- "They were *passionate* and made very complex concepts simple to understand."

- "They were able to *personally relate* their topic to the things that keep me awake at night."

- "Their *personal stories* gave more insight into them as people and helped me trust their leadership more."

There's a relational thread throughout these responses. Do you see it? Capturing the hearts and minds of busy people today demands we understand them at a deeper level. Good leaders must know how to read the moment and, at times, take their communication to a place better-suited to motivate the human heart—the right part of the brain.

When material is presented in the form of stories, people interaction and discussion, vivid relational experiences, or visual aids, it is most often assimilated on the right side of the brain, which is responsible for processing more relational/emotional stimulus. That's why we need to become multi-dimensional communicators and tap into the power of right-brain communication.

We will remember something we've held in our hands, a powerful feeling we've experienced in a group, or a leader's personal story for months or even years. We will most likely not remember any of the bullet points delivered just an hour earlier.

As Maya Angelou once reminded us, *"People will never remember what you say, but they will always remember how you made them feel."*

At its essence, every communication opportunity is simply a well-told story, a story of challenge, a story of accomplishment or innovation, or perhaps a story of how the last quarter impacted your company's plans for the future. And whether you've fallen into leadership or aspired to it your entire life, you may choose how that story is best told. Those who understand how to orchestrate the critical balance of factual, relational, and symbolic communication will be rewarded with passionate followers and amazing results.

Jim Endicott is president of Distinction Communication Inc. (www.distinction-services.com), a Newberg, Oregon, consulting firm specializing in message development, presentation design, and delivery skills coaching.

• • •

GOOD AUDIENCE INTERACTIVITY AS PART OF YOUR STYLE
Dianna Booher

PEOPLE INTERACT WITH THEIR computers, DVDs, iPads, cell phones, home security systems, ATMs, and airline check-in systems. Team members give 360-degree feedback to their peers and supervisors. They send suggestions to the senior executives by e-mail. Suppliers survey clients to ask, "How are we doing?"

So when it comes to presentations, audiences assume that you will build in a two-way dialogue and interactivity—that you will not simply provide an information dump and walk away, thinking you have communicated and achieved your objective.

Not only do today's audiences demand interactivity, but also you as presenter will find that it serves some useful purposes of your own: Interactivity helps cement key points. It provides a change of pace and gives audiences a chance to "catch their breath" almost as much as a physical break.

Interactivity can add levity to the atmosphere and also help you to build rapport. And depending on which techniques you choose, interactivity can "break the ice" among audience members and encourage them to get to know each other.

Neither do audience-involvement techniques necessarily need to be time-consuming or complex. In fact, some audience-involvement techniques do not even require your audience to speak at all. For example, just calling an audience member's name grabs his or her attention and says to the rest of the group: "I'm aware of you as individuals, with specific needs, issues, and concerns."

Use the "Reveal" Technique

Chart after chart of PowerPoint data can be deadly. For variety, create an opportunity to make your information "stick" with your listeners. For example, instead of telling them what the accuracy rate was on filling orders last quarter, have them guess the percentage. Then reveal the actual statistic.

Instead of telling them how successful the marketing campaign in the second quarter was, ask them to guess how many leads it generated as compared with other typical campaigns. Then ask them to guess the spike in sales during the first thirty days after the marketing campaign. Then reveal the numbers.

The best guessers likely will get a kick out of patting themselves on the back. And the poor guessers will be truly surprised. In both cases, the numbers will make a much greater impact than had you simply reported them.

Tell a "Hero Story" Involving an Audience Member

Audiences like to participate vicariously as you recognize one of their own: "It seems that every division has one person who stands out as a mentor. Joan Gandee is her division's mentor" tends to make the group glance at Joan and think for themselves about their own mentors while you tell Joan's story.

You can discover such anecdotes as you research your audience. For example, if you are talking about the need to improve customer service in your organization, as you investigate you undoubtedly will hear a few stories about those who provide exceptional service. Tell their stories in a specific situation as the model to strive for with all customers.

Ask for Audience Examples or Experiences

A question such as "Can anyone give me an example of this principle of ethics at work in your community or organization?" customizes your point for a particular audience.

Make sure, however, that your group does have experiences to share. Otherwise you are left with dead silence, making you look as though either you do not know your audience or they are bored with the topic. To prevent the dead silence, you can solicit volunteers ahead of time or simply make sure that you are aware of key people to call on who are willing to provide examples or experiences.

Do be aware, however, of the danger of opening the floor to others. They may take longer than expected to tell their stories. They may change the mood of your presentation. Or they may provide an example that contradicts your point.

Ask the Audience to Brainstorm or Create Lists

Listing creates quick awareness in a more interactive way than lecturing. Brainstorming promotes creative thinking about possibilities—you may or may not want to lead the group to a conclusion about which of the ideas is best. If you have participants call out the ideas or items as one large group, you may or may not want someone to write them down so that you can refer to them later.

If they make a list in small groups, you may ask all, a few, or only one team to call out their list at the conclusion of the activity. If one group reports their output, you can have other groups add only items or ideas not mentioned by the first.

Involve Your Audience Early

Audiences become set in their moods early. Signal your expectations clearly up-front to create an atmosphere of "we're in this together" to make your time together beneficial.

By instructing audience members to "Turn to the person on your left and give a thirty-second description of your part in the project," you add variety and a personal touch to your overview.

Provide Only a General Agenda

When you provide a specific topic outline, you limit your flexibility if you decide to alter your timetable to adjust to the interests of your group, to accept new issues raised by the group, or to accommodate other unexpected situations.

Additionally, some people feel cheated that you did not cover certain points listed on the agenda. You often will receive comments and questions such as: "You skipped the part about X! What about that? It says here that you planned to cover that."

Instead, select one of these options: (1) list broad topic areas only, omitting all references to timing or (2) use a graphic design that omits any semblance of chronology but instead displays specifics in random order, size, and intensity.

Provide an Emotionally Safe Environment

Dominating audience members can quickly "shut down" timid ones. Impatient participants can rush talkers so that they feel inhibited about speaking up with an experience, example, or question.

It is easy for presenters to focus on the body language and comments of the more vocal in the group and not notice that others have withdrawn. As the leader of a group interaction, a key task is equalizing the personalities to the degree that all feel comfortable to speak.

If things go wrong—if a long-winded person dominates, if someone feels embarrassed, if someone feels that he or she had no opportunity for input, if someone is bored—audience members will blame you. You are the host of your presentation.

Make People Feel Smart, Not Stupid

This principle particularly holds true in training sessions. Help participants master concepts and grow in self-confidence as they move through the session, rather than making them feel overwhelmed and deficient. Although they may leave admiring your knowledge, they will not likely move any closer to the learning objective.

In an informative presentation, rather than a game of "gotcha" while you reveal little-known data and decisions, it is typically better to lead your audience along with you toward conclusions by educating them as you go. That is, explain terms, criteria, processes, and reasoning. As they understand more about the subject, they likely will move closer to the goal.

Make Participation Optional

Keep in mind that audience participation works best when everyone has a choice. Pressure to participate—even to raise a hand in response to a question—may intimidate or even irritate some.

You can prevent most hesitancy by knowing your audience and always selecting appropriate interactivity to accomplish your purpose. Your enthusiastic participation encourages others. In short, be your own cheerleader, but do not ask the audience to do anything that makes them uncomfortable.

Dianna Booher is the CEO of Booher Consultants (www.booher.com) in Dallas, Texas, and works with organizations to increase their productivity and effectiveness through better oral, written, interpersonal, and cross-functional communication.

• • •

CALCULATING THE REAL COST OF POOR PRESENTATIONS
Dave Paradi

WE HAVE ALL SEEN them—poorly designed or delivered presentations. The ones where the PowerPoint slides were unreadable, the presenter stood facing the screen and read each slide as it was displayed, and the audience's key information needs weren't addressed. These presentations are frustrating to watch, but more importantly, cost organizations a huge amount of money.

The costs of a poor sales presentation include a longer purchasing decision cycle, requests for more information before a purchase is made, and ultimately, a smaller sale or no sale at all. The costs of a poor internal presentation include delayed decisions, more meetings to clarify the issue, additional information being requested, incorrect decisions, and sometimes a negative impact on one's career.

The dollar cost of poor sales presentations is easier to calculate because the largest component is the lost revenue. The dollar cost of a poor internal presentation, on the other hand, is harder to calculate because we don't see it show up on a sales report.

Even though it is harder to calculate, it's important to consider. The dollar costs of a poor internal presentation are primarily contained in the extra time that people spend because the message wasn't clear the first time.

Examples of this extra time include the hours spent doing extra research, preparing additional documentation, more one-on-one discussions, more time spent in group meetings to clarify the original message, and more time spent reviewing additional documentation.

When we add up the number of staff hours spent on all of these tasks, it is not surprising to find that it is ten or more hours for each poor presentation.

At that rate, the dollar costs add up quickly.

One Organization's Costs

Let me use an organization I met with recently as an example. This is a medium-sized organization with approximately eight hundred full-time employees. When we sat down, I asked them about the problem and they estimated that there are at least forty to fifty internal presentations each week and that about 25 percent require additional work because the presentation was not done well.

At the rate of ten hours of extra staff time per poor presentation and a professional staff salary of $50,000 per year, the cost to this organization is over $133,000 per year!

You can easily calculate how much poor presentations are costing your own department or organization. Start by estimating the number of internal presentations that are done per week. Include management briefings, customer presentations, project updates, staff meetings, and other presentations. This number is usually higher than we thought it would be.

Then, estimate what percentage of those presentations are done poorly, resulting in additional work. In most organizations this can be in the 25 to 40 percent range. Next, guesstimate the amount of staff time spent in clarifying the poor presentations. Include the hours spent on additional research, extra documentation, more meetings, and reviews. It is not unusual to find this is ten to fifteen hours per poor presentation.

Finally, find out what the average salary is of a staff member doing the extra work. Now, use the following formula to calculate the total cost to your organization of poor internal presentations:

Annual Cost of Poor Presentations = # of presentations per week X 52 weeks per year X % of poor presentations X # hours extra work required X Hourly Salary Factor (see approximations below).

Salary Factor Table

Average Annual Salary

$35,000	=	$17.95 per hour
$40,000	=	$20.51 per hour
$45,000	=	$23.08
$50,000	=	$25.64
$55,000	=	$28.21

When you see the real cost to your organization of substandard presentations, you will be much more willing to invest in training to help reduce the number of poor presentations.

What's Causing Shoddy Presentations?

The bigger question remains: What is the primary cause of these poor presentations?

In my experience it is a misuse of PowerPoint. Too many people use it as a magical crutch that will somehow substitute for proper preparation of a presentation. Consider these three tips to help improve your organization's presentations.

First, define the goal of the presentation and plan how it will move the audience from where they are now to where you want them to be. Second, develop your PowerPoint slides so that they enhance your message, not detract from it. And finally, if you have prepared properly, you will know your material so well that you can deliver your presentation as a conversation instead of simply reading each slide as it is displayed.

Just imagine the productivity gains in your organization possible by reducing the number of poorly designed or delivered internal presentations.

Dave Paradi runs the Think Outside the Slide website (www.thinkoutsidetheslide .com), is a consultant on high-stakes presentations, author of seven books, and a Microsoft PowerPoint Most Valuable Professional (MVP).

3

Perfect Practice

MAXIMIZING YOUR REHEARSAL TIME

Understanding the difference between practice and rehearsal can determine whether your presentation makes a lasting impact or falls flat with audiences. Practice—sitting in your office or on an airplane reviewing PowerPoint slides—isn't rehearsal. Rehearsal means being up on your feet, using the same gestures, eye contact, pacing, and interaction with technology you would in the actual presentation.

Most presenters spend their limited rehearsal time reviewing bullet points on slides and other visuals—content that audiences can see and read for themselves. But experts believe it's better to allocate even more rehearsal time to the *invisible* content—transitions between slides, personal stories, analogies, and elaboration of slide text.

Those elements of a speech that shine the appropriate spotlight on you the presenter, not on your slides, ultimately determine how well your message will be received and retained by audiences.

• • •

EIGHT GUIDELINES FOR PERFECT PRESENTATION PRACTICE
Marjorie Brody

WHEN IT COMES TO presenting, does practice make perfect? In a word, no. Practice makes *permanent*.

Your goal should be to practice perfectly, not just practice. The more you do something, the more comfortable it feels—whether right or wrong. So we need to do it right when we practice our presentations.

Knowing a subject doesn't guarantee presentation success. The ability to articulate the message and connect with audience members is what counts—and perfect practice can make this happen.

Practice Works for Me

A personal example that proves perfect practice works is a recent sales presentation that I was asked to deliver regarding my company's professional development capabilities. After structuring my presentation, I first presented it to one of my account managers. She had a few suggestions, including that I start with a story.

After I updated my presentation, I practiced it with one of our facilitators, who came to the meeting with me. She suggested that I make the presentation more interactive and more responsive to the client's specific needs and worked with me to do that. We also practiced ways that she could facilitate some of the discussion.

Our practice not only included segues between the two of us—to ensure they were smooth—but also practice related to our timing. We even discussed where we would each be sitting in the room to get the maximum involvement from the audience! During our car ride to the client site in New York, we practiced it three more times.

When we arrived, we were ready, we had anticipated the audience's questions, the timing worked, and best news of all—we obtained results (we made the sale).

Practice Will Work for You, Too

Winging a presentation rarely achieves the desired results. Here is the approach that works for me—dare I say—100 percent of the time. My assumption is that you have done the preparation:

- Know your PAL (Purpose, Audience, and Logistics).

- Collect current, accurate, and relevant information.

- Add examples, stories, emotional appeals, and some visuals when critical to support the data.

- Organize materials so there is a logical flow of content, with smooth transitions connecting the ideas—creating a story.

- Have a strong opening and close already written.

- Create a user-friendly final draft, making it easy to reference without reading it.

Frequently, presenters do all of the above, and then think through presentations in their minds, where we are all amazingly eloquent. Visualizing is great, but it doesn't replace the actual out-loud practice.

Too frequently, practice is left until close to the date of a presentation—when it's too late. The goal of practice sessions is to get presenters totally comfortable with the content, the slides, and the timing so that, when they actually present, they are able to concentrate on connecting with the audience.

Eight Guidelines for Presentation Practice

Here are my eight guidelines for perfect practice:

1. **Practice out loud.** Say the presentation out loud; three to six times should do it.

2. **Practice with variety.** Every time you say your presentation, say it differently. The goal is to keep it conversational, not memorize exact phrases.

3. **Be aware of timing.** Leave time in your practice session for audience interaction, questions, and so forth.

4. **Practice in front of a real audience, similar to your target audience.** Practice in front of people who are similar to the "real audience." If there are words that you are using they don't understand or concepts that aren't clear, it's better to find out in front of this group rather than in front of the "real audience."

5. **Incorporate spontaneous Q&A into your practice.** If you anticipate fielding questions or being interrupted during the presentation, make sure your practice audience is doing the same.

6. **Spend more time on the speech opening and closing.** Practice your opening and close more frequently—commute time is great for this.

7. **Practice your timing.** If the entire presentation is to last for thirty minutes, the practice should go no longer than eighteen to twenty-five minutes, depending on the amount of interaction or number of questions you anticipate.

8. **Practice by recording yourself.** If they are very critical presentations, videotape yourself.

An executive I coach from a large pharmaceutical company had a large "town hall" meeting coming up—to introduce company policy changes. He knew that the audience would be anxious, and in some cases hostile. When we first discussed the outline for his presentation, it was very data-driven. In no way was he getting in touch with the emotions that people were feeling.

Once we changed the structure of his presentation, he began to practice and to "own" the material.

After the meeting, he told me that, due to this practice, he was comfortable in the delivery, totally in the moment—resonating both emotionally and psychologically with the audience. He now insists that all of his direct reports use the eight practice guidelines that I coached him on.

From my perspective, practice isn't fun. But there is no substitute for it. Keep in mind what management consultant Peter Drucker said: "Spontaneity is an infinite number of rehearsed possibilities."

Marjorie Brody is the head of BRODY Professional Development (www.brodypro .com), which provides training programs, executive coaching, and presentations in the area of presentations power, facilitation, and meeting effectiveness. Brody also is the author of more than twenty books and is a member of the CPAE Speaker Hall of Fame.

• • •

SEVEN SECRETS TO PSYCH YOURSELF OUT OF PRE-PRESENTATION JITTERS
Dianna Booher

STAGE FRIGHT OFTEN BEGINS long before a performer takes the stage. For most of us, the condition sets in the moment we accept an invitation to make a presentation. And generally, the longer we have to anticipate the event, the more prolonged and severe the symptoms.

The typical person is uncomfortable in a presentation forum. Neither rank nor personality is a differentiator. In years of coaching on presentation skills, I have had some of the most outstanding executives tell me that they still feel uncomfortable in front of a group—even after hundreds of presentations before employee, stockholder, or industry groups.

And even life-of-the-party-type salespeople who give a great presentation sometimes walk away with sweaty palms and knots in their stomachs. The following hints may help you deal with that sense of discomfort until it dissolves into confidence.

Secret 1: Accept Nervousness as Part of the Process

At times our fears are rational; sometimes not. We may fear that our subject or information is not quite what the audience expects, needs, or wants. Or we fear that they will attack the quality of our performance or challenge our credentials, asking a question we cannot answer. Or we visualize ourselves making a misstatement or omitting key information.

Even if we know our subject well and feel confident about our qualifications to speak, we may fear that we will perform so badly that we will embarrass ourselves. Surely the group will notice our nervousness and our embarrassment.

If we have no other cause for fear, some of us worry that we won't have adequate preparation time or that some circumstance beyond our control (such as the audiovisual equipment going berserk) will foul things up.

If any of these are fears of yours, you are in good company. Even the most famous movie stars, singers, and politicians admit to fear before certain performances. When you hear someone claim not to be nervous before giving a presentation, you are probably in for a boring talk.

Presenters who lack a certain amount of anxiety do not have enough adrenaline flow to push them to peak performance. They are too confident and relaxed to do their best jobs.

Secret 2: Use Fear to Push Yourself to Peak Performance

The secret to a great presentation is performing despite the nervousness—in fact, making your jitters work for you. Imagine the tension and extra adrenalin pumping through you as catalysts to a great performance.

You may feel that you have lost control of your body, with one of the following symptoms: rapid pulse, sweaty palms, dry mouth, buckling knees, twitching muscles, shortness of breath, quivering voice, and queasiness.

No matter how nervous you are, however, never tell your audience. If they sense your discomfort, they will worry about you—much like a parent does when a daughter mounts the school stage as Cinderella. Your admission may direct them to your shaking hands when they should be listening to your words.

Take a deep breath and refuse to let your nerves get the best of you. Instead of thinking about how you might embarrass yourself, concentrate on your subject. Recall and rehearse your key points rather than your key obstacles.

Use positive self-talk rather than focusing on the fear. One way to build your confidence is to remember that you have been asked to give the presentation; someone believes in your capability and subject-matter expertise. Remind yourself that if others in the audience were more knowledgeable than you, they would have been asked to make the presentation.

Fear is a learned response. A two-year-old does not fear walking into the street until someone yanks him or her back, warning of the danger. We learn the same fear of speaking before a group the first time a classmate stands up to recite a poem, has a memory lapse, and becomes flustered, causing snickers to erupt throughout the room.

And because fear is learned, it can be unlearned—or at least controlled.

Secret 3: Find Your Fans

It is part of human nature to be cowed by negative personality types. This goes for presenters also. They look into the audience and see the one glum face staring at them, looking bored, angry, or impatient. The tendency is to play to that one cynic, trying to persuade, soften, lead, motivate, empower, enlighten, or appease— whatever it takes to turn the gloom to bloom.

However, it rarely happens. And in the process, you grow more nervous and rattled and sometimes lose the rest of the audience.

It is far better to find your fans up-front. If you know you have supportive people in the group, focus on those faces. These positive high achievers sport a different expression. They smile. They blink.

They nod. They move. They shift. They are the let's-keep-an-open-mind, let's-make-this-work kind of people.

They do not just suck the energy out of you—they give some back. These people have a contagious spirit that generates enthusiasm for at least a discussion, if not acceptance, of your ideas.

Secret 4: Play Mental Games of "What's the Worst?" to Overcome Disabling Fear

Another trick for calming yourself is to consider the unnerving experience in light of eternity. What is the worst that can happen? What will it all matter a year from now? In fact, if you goof, who will even remember it tomorrow?

In the big scheme of things, your presentation will prove minuscule. Plan, then learn to put the unexpected in perspective.

Secret 5: Use Physical Exercise to Release Nervous Tension

Following are some things you can do to alleviate both the physical and mental symptoms of nervousness:

- Take a few deep breaths and exhale slowly. (This forces the muscles to relax a bit, increases the flow of oxygen to the brain, and lowers the pulse rate.)
- Let all the muscles in your body go limp, then tense them, and then let them go limp again.
- Drop your jaw and move it from side to side. Yawn.
- Roll your head, shoulders, or both.
- Go limp like Raggedy Ann and then straighten up. Repeat.
- Take a brisk walk or jog before arriving at the event.

The idea is to transport yourself from terror to fear to tension to mere stimulation. It is in the stimulation mode that you will be best able to inspire or motivate your audience.

Secret 6: Concentrate on Your Audience Rather Than on Yourself

How will your ideas help your audience to improve their lives, take action at work, or at least increase their knowledge? Learn to appreciate the energy this tension creates; think of the swarm of butterflies in your stomach as a wellspring of creativity pushing upward to make your presentation one to remember. Feel passionate about your subject. Prepare well. Psych yourself up for the positive results your presentation is sure to generate.

Secret 7: Assume a Friendly Audience

If you assume the members of your audience are waiting to catch you in an error or argue with you, you'll likely feel nervous and may even sound hostile during your presentation.

Based on my own experience and that of many other professional speakers, I assure you that audiences want speakers to do well. After all, they have taken time out of their busy schedules, and they are hoping to gain something from your presentation. Even those who are forced to attend will be pleasantly surprised if you give them something of value or entertain them.

To reassure yourself that your audience members are friendly and positive, arrive early and talk with people individually. Chat about the occasion, their trip to the site, what their work entails, common acquaintances—anything that lets them see you as a nice person who is interested in them. Such small talk also allows you to see them as familiar "friends" who will welcome and benefit from what you have to say.

Even your body language conveys how you feel about your audience. If you feel that they are friendly, you will walk over and stand closer to them. If you are uncomfortable with them, you will hide behind the lectern or table and lean away.

Finally, do not be discouraged by frowns or silences. *Silence means deep thought and agreement as often as it does boredom.* With this perspective, your delivery will sound relaxed and upbeat.

Don't Let Fear Mean Mediocrity

Finally, don't settle for being an "average" presenter, one who is scared into conformity. Do not risk losing your audience with a boringly straitlaced performance—one that is not too passionate, not too loud, not too flashy, not too funny, not too controversial, not too emotional, not too formal, not too informal—not too anything. Never look around your organization to see "what everybody else does" when they present and conform to mediocrity.

See what everyone else does, and do not do it. Your success depends more often on being different—on standing out as superior. Relax and excel.

Dianna Booher is CEO of Booher Consultants Inc. (www.booher.com) and works with organizations to increase their productivity and effectiveness through better oral, written, interpersonal, and cross-functional communication.

• • •

IS IT PRACTICE . . . OR REHEARSAL?
David Zielinski

IF YOU'RE LIKE MANY speakers, the end of a presentation signals the start of your brilliant insight. If only I hadn't stumbled over that key phrase. If only I had handled that question a bit more deftly or found more compelling data to support my message. And of course, one of the most common post-presentation laments, *If only I'd had more time to practice.*

The truth is, no amount of preparation time is enough. Allot one month to develop and practice for a big speech and, in the post-mortem, you'll wish it had been two. Set aside two weeks, and later you think four would have been better. Or the three nights you spend burning the midnight oil should have been five.

This inevitable time crunch is partly a function of Parkinson's Law ("work expands to fill the time available for its completion") and partly a result of speakers' perfectionist tendencies. According to many presentation skill coaches, it's also an indictment of the preparation process most speakers go through.

Prep time is always scarce, say experts, so how you use that precious time—and in many cases whether you understand the distinction between *practice* and *rehearsal*—is what makes the difference between a mediocre presentation and a memorable one.

Is It Practice . . . or Rehearsal?

Think for a moment about your own preparation routine. Let's say you have your text, PowerPoint slides, and handouts in good shape and have begun practicing delivery. If you're like most busy presenters, you practice on your commute, by stealing time in your office, on the couch, or at home.

And therein lies the problem, experts say: Too much time in practice and not enough in rehearsal. Rehearsal means being up on your feet, using the same gestures, eye contact, pacing, and interaction with PowerPoint or Prezi you will in your actual presentation. Practice—sitting on an airplane or in your office reviewing scripts or slides—isn't rehearsal.

Rehearsal requires getting your mind off content and onto connecting with an audience. Too often speakers overwork *what* they are going to say during practice, and under-work *how* they're going to say it during rehearsal. As one presentation skill coach says, "If it were only about the material, we could simply e-mail presentations to audiences and have them e-mail questions back."

Managing Your Media

Equally important is how you rehearse with your media. For many, rehearsal means reviewing bulleted text points and using PowerPoint slides, in effect, as cue cards. The problem comes in spending too much time on this "visible" content—that which the audience can see and read for themselves—at the expense of rehearsing "invisible" content, such as slide transitions, personal stories, or analogies.

Power of Revision

It's been said that all good writing is rewriting. The true power of concise, compelling, and colorful language is arrived at in the revision process, not in your script's creation, so spend even more time in rewrite than in first drafts. Experts also suggest trying to make three points that stick, rather than ten points that leave no lasting impression.

While you want your key messages and slides in tip-top shape, you also don't want to let precious hours slip away by obsessing over word choice or phrasing, especially since your actual speech will vary from your scripted notes. In most cases, content is ready before speakers think it is, allowing you to shift more quickly into rehearsing the delivery.

Rethinking Your Visual Prep

Another place presenters tend to use their preparation time unwisely is in creating their PowerPoint slides, either by spending too much time on too many slides or not spending enough time to prepare even modestly competent slides.

No one wants to be creating or editing PowerPoint slides in the panicky last hours before a presentation, so it's important to set aside enough time for the task—but not too much time. For those inexperienced with the software, some experts suggest allotting at least one hour of development time per electronic slide, which includes time for initial design and text revision. The pros, of course, can crank out finished versions much more quickly.

Of course, what you choose to put on slides also is critical, and this can potentially save or waste time, depending on your approach. Some speech coaches suggest asking yourself, "How many bulleted text slides could I replace with something more visually stimulating that will get my audience thinking about the same point?"

Besides making presentations more compelling, visually oriented approaches that substitute art or other pre-made graphics for bulleted text can save speakers time and force them to focus on other skills that most often raise a presentation from mediocre to memorable: spontaneity, audience interaction, and mastering the material, not just memorizing it.

David Zielinski is the editor of PresentationXpert newsletter (www.presentation-xpert.com). This article was adapted from an article that first appeared in *Toastmaster* magazine.

• • •

REPETITIONS AND REPUTATIONS
Jim Endicott

A FEW YEARS BACK I was cajoled by some buddies to be in a golf tournament with them. First of all, I never golf enough to really improve. And if I had thought for a second, I would have realized their motivation wasn't to just hang out with a good friend for a few hours, it was to wax my sorry....

But they underestimated a deeply rooted competitive streak in me. So a week before the big tournament I scheduled a golf lesson to fix what was, until then, a mild slice. It meant that when others were playing in the sun and enjoying the fairway, I was usually searching for my ball in the woods.

The golf pro showed up, and I was pretty excited. A few quick fixes and I'd be good to go! (I hear a few of you chuckling already.) During the course of the next sixty minutes, I would have a number of things "corrected." First my stance. Then my swing path. And finally my hips and my head.

One hour and $75 later, my mild slice had morphed into what golfers affectionately refer to as a "duck hook." I'll save you the description. Suffice it to say it's not very pretty and now meant I would not only be playing in the woods, but most likely the next fairway over.

Power of Continuous Improvement

What happened to me is what happens to many presenters today.

They obtain a little presentation skills coaching, feel some momentary discomfort because their existing habits are so deeply entrenched, and then abandon their important new skill set before it can effectively take root. (The same skills, by the way, that others admired so much at the end of their training day.) For this reason, far too many presenters never move to the level they aspire to and the presentation process has just become a necessary evil.

But from time to time we're reminded of what can happen when someone is willing to lean into this important life skill. One of our executive trainers, Fred, was back in Boston working with a senior manager at a global sporting apparel company. Every time we were in town, this manager had requested a personal coaching session with us.

Because he was so bad and desperately needed the help? To the contrary, because he was so exceptionally *good* as a communicator.

When we asked him why he kept signing up for personal coaching, his answer was refreshing. He had been a professional tennis coach at one point in his life and knew first-hand that it took a *thousand conscious repetitions* of a new movement before it became second-nature. "That's why I keep coming back—to get more reps."

There's a lesson in this for anyone who aspires to be an exceptional communicator.

If you've had some personal coaching, are you applying the skills at every opportunity or do you just expect them to magically show up on presentation day? If you haven't received training in this critical area, are you willing? If you are passionate about being the kind of presenter who is remembered at the end of a very long day, take to heart what every professional understands about the nature of meaningful personal change.

You've got to want it.

You've got to commit to it for the long run.

You've got to believe that the benefits of mastery are well worth the time and effort to get there.

Jim Endicott is president of Distinction Communication Inc. (www.distinction-services.com), a Newberg, Oregon, consulting firm specializing in message development, presentation design, and delivery skills coaching.

• • •

SECRETS TO PRACTICING YOUR PRESENTATION WHEN YOU HAVE NO TIME
Michelle Mazur

WE KNOW WE HAVE to practice, but practice seems like an abstract, daunting task. The biggest objection I hear from clients about practicing a presentation is "*I don't have time to practice.*" I understand the problem. I don't have time to practice my presentations either . . . and frankly, I am the type of presenter who does not enjoy practicing at all. My little hater comes out in full force! Let's go through step-by-step and discuss some strategies that will save you time.

Step One: Divvy Up Your Presentation into Bite-Size Chunks

If you are doing a thirty-, sixty-, or even ninety-minute speech, you do *not* have to practice your presentation all at once. Repeat: you do *not* have to rehearse your entire presentation in one sitting. Break up your presentation in small bite-size chunks. Divide it up by introduction, each main point, and your conclusion.

If it is a longer presentation, break the body of the speech down into its sub-points. Think of this as portion control for practicing your speech. It makes practice less daunting.

Step Two: Find Small Chunks of Time to Practice

Now that you know that you don't have to practice the presentation all at once, start finding pockets of time for small practice sessions. This means driving in your car is a great time to practice. Ten minutes between calls—practice. Taking a shower—forget singing—try practicing.

There's all kinds of time to practice when you don't have to find a huge chunk of time.

Step Three: Don't Always Start from the Beginning

You need to know your introduction well! However, don't always start your rehearsals at the beginning. Every time you are practicing, think about what you need to go over the most. In which part of the presentation is the information most difficult for you? Which part of the speech have you not practiced yet? Start there.

Step Four: Practice Does Not Always Have to Be Out Loud

Practicing your speech out loud is a must. However, you don't always have to practice out loud. Visualization is a form of practicing. Going through the speech in your head is a way to rehearse. Even if you just want to write the speech out—guess what? You are practicing.

Step Five: Do One Complete Run Through with Technology

You have to find the time to do at least one complete run through with your tech (microphone, PowerPoint, media). This ensures that you are staying within the time limits, your transitions are good, and that all your technology is in working order.

Dr. Michelle Mazur (www.drmichellemazur.com) is a public speaking coach, communication expert, and author of the Relationally Speaking blog.

4

Tapping PowerPoint's Hidden Potential

If Microsoft's PowerPoint isn't the most polarizing business software on the planet, it's near the top of the list. Many presenters treat PowerPoint as a life support system, unable to conceive how they could survive without it, while just as many others see the software as a scourge to the presentations field for the questionable slide design practices it encourages through its underlying programming and templates.

Yet, like any such tool, PowerPoint's impact ultimately lies in how it is positioned and used within presentations. Employ it as a poor-man's teleprompter—creating and then reading lengthy bullet points verbatim to audiences—and you contribute to PowerPoint's bad name. But use it instead in ways that complement or enhance a core spoken message—with compelling headlines, spare use of text, powerful photos, or elucidating graphics—and PowerPoint can vastly improve an audience's ability to embrace and retain key messages.

In this chapter we've compiled some of the best slide design tips, insider shortcuts, and perspectives for using PowerPoint's features in ways that help the software live up to its often-unfulfilled promise.

• • •

CULTIVATING A HEALTHY RELATIONSHIP WITH YOUR SLIDES

Nancy Duarte

THERE'S NOT MUCH ON this planet more gratifying than being in a healthy and comfortable relationship. My husband and I often use the metaphor of a steamboat to describe our interaction: I'm the one above the surface, sputtering, churning, and making noise to create propulsion, and he's the quiet rudder under the surface providing guidance and wisdom to make sure we don't run aground.

I would describe our relationship as interdependent. We're reliant upon and respectful of what the other brings to the partnership, and that's what makes it successful. But how would you characterize the relationship you have with your visual aids? What metaphor would you use to describe it? Actor and stage? Or drug and dealer?

When you present, are you codependent, interdependent, or even independent of your PowerPoint slides? The term "codependent" was coined in the mid 1980s and initially used by Alcoholics Anonymous to describe the unhealthy psychological condition that occurs in a relationship when one partner suffers from an addiction. A codependent person ends up providing too much care—and often too much latitude—to someone who is unhealthy.

You are in a codependent relationship with your slides if you are desperately addicted to them and unable to break away. You may even make excuses for their sad condition, which, of course, only perpetuates their dilapidated state.

If you are in a work culture that enables this codependent relationship, it will be even tougher to transform yourself. *The first step is to admit you have a problem. The second is to acknowledge that your slides have become unmanageable.*

The Dense-Slide Addiction

Dense content on slides can be addictive. The default template settings in applications such as PowerPoint encourage us to put an enormous amount of text on each slide, which transforms the slide into a document rather than a visual aid.

The slides take on the role of teleprompter, requiring us to read them to the audience instead of connecting with our listeners. This habit requires little or no effort on the part of presenters to rehearse; they simply need to read aloud along with the audience.

Thus, instead of becoming true "carriers" of our content, we are happy to merely repeat our own words. Although definitely the easiest and quickest way to present—it requires no effort on your part other than writing the presentation—*is it really best for your audience?*

It's frustrating to sit through a presentation, reading bullet points, waiting for the presenter to catch up as he or she expounds on the already very thorough and dense text. We can read, you know.

Using this media improperly creates the impression that the presentation is solely about the slides and the presenter and not about the audience's comprehension or insights. Originally, slides were intended to be a visual aid for the audience, a mnemonic device to help them retain and recall the material being presented.

Slides are like the stage in a play or the costume for the actor; they are not themselves the star of the show, but they do provide the context and setting in which you can give a memorable performance.

So what can we do for ourselves if we're trapped in a codependent relationship with our slides that negatively impacts our audiences? Garr Reynolds of Presentation Zen says that the concept of "restrictions as liberators" can be applied to almost any presentation situation.

By placing constraints and restrictions on ourselves and our media, we can break our codependent relationships, although it will take hard work and commitment.

Constrain the Text

Letting go of slides-as-crutch is a process that requires time, patience, and practice. Possibly the biggest issue facing presenters is that *they don't take the time to rehearse.* Think about what a performance would be like if the actors skimmed though the play the night before: it would suck.

Actors spend hours memorizing their scripts and hours more practicing their delivery. That's why they're effective. Except for me, that is. During sixth-grade summer school I took a theater class and was rewarded for being the last to sign up with the lead role in the play. Instructed to memorize all thirty-six of my lines, I dutifully attempted to fulfill my task without the benefit of being guided to read the entire play, learn the overarching story line, and appreciate the other characters.

Rather, I focused on my lines only and remained lost and confused all summer. The plan was to perform the play in front of the entire student body, but we had to have a "special private performance" because of me. Although there are several lines from that play that will be etched in my mind forever, to this day I have no idea what the play was about.

I didn't capture the spirit of the story or the meaning of the content. I never ingested it to the point of owning it. In the end, I couldn't let go of the playbook and needed to carry it around on stage.

If only I had been given insights into how to ingest content to make it seem natural.

Experimenting with letting go of text and slide junk might be hard at first. That's because when you were writing your presentation you carefully put all those hundreds of visual triggers on your slides as you formulated the structure and content.

As a safety net, you relied on all those triggers so you would remember to keep your story straight and not screw up your own play. But all those superfluous words and clutter affect your audience's experience.

Removing clutter is a process, one that will take courage, practice, time, and lots of trial and error before you feel the benefits of being free. You might slip, fall, and initially exude more nervous energy when you present, but it will cause your presentations to be more about your connection with the audience and less about the slides.

Here are the Three R's of text removal on slides:

1. **Reduce:** Practice presenting with your slides a few times. Then highlight only one key word per bullet point. Practice delivering those slides again, but focus only on the highlighted word. The other words will still be there, so you can reference them if needed. Once you can deliver the slides from the key words, remove all the words on the slides except for the key words and present from that. Ideally, it's best to then replace that word with an image when possible.

2. **Record:** Many people are auditory learners. Read your script or present your slides out loud and record the delivery. Play the recording during your commute or close your eyes and listen to it before you go to bed. Once you get past hearing the sound of your own voice, you'll be able to absorb the content and will feel comfortable reducing the clutter on your slides.

3. **Repeat:** Read your script and/or slides out loud several times and then close your eyes and repeat the content over and over. In other words, tell yourself your story. Refine it. Get past those stumbling blocks. Then look at your slides and delete as much text and junk as you can while remembering the key points that need to be made.

Constrain the Length

Have you ever finished a presentation and had folks flock to you begging you to make it longer next time? Probably not. Attention spans are getting shorter and shorter. Thirty-minute sitcoms, five-minute YouTube videos, and fifteen-second commercials all influence the duration of our attention spans.

And that short span takes into account that TV and Internet media are usually professionally prepared and most often geared to entertain. So when the content isn't emotionally stimulating but is still crucial and necessary to effective communication, you can enhance the impact by packing a punch in a smaller time slot. Dragging the audience down Dullard Lane isn't anyone's favorite afternoon trip.

Constraining your presentation's length forces you to be concise and remove anything superfluous to the message. Proof in point is TED, the annual conference featuring some of the greatest thought leaders and innovators in the world, which helps spread ideas and shape our culture and future.

Each of these phenomenal presenters communicates his or her idea in eighteen minutes or less. If some of the most influential people in the world can deliver powerful content in eighteen minutes, so can you. Just try boiling it down.

For internal company meetings, constraining presentations and reserving some of the meeting for conversation, ideation, and Q&A would be refreshing. Some companies are beginning to constrain the number of slides allowed and encouraging a rapid-fire approach so that more insights can be shared in a single setting.

Can You Go PowerPoint-Less?

Now we're ready to share what a relationship can be like independent of slides. *Is it possible to deliver a presentation without any slides?* Consider what would happen to your presentation if there were a power outage. Evaluating and rejecting bad habits that have formed as a result of reliance on presentation software is critical to your success. It will force you to take ownership of the content in your head and heart.

Several ways to use visual aids don't involve a projector. Flip charts, props, handouts, flip books, and even physical devices work if you have a small audience. Using more tactile forms of communication with a small audience increases your humanness.

On the other hand, if you are in a large venue with a projector, you can increase your presence by pressing the B key on the keyboard.

This will turn your screen to black, forcing your audience to focus on you. (Alternately, the W key will change your screen to white.)

If your keyboard is out of range, slip an all-black slide into your deck. This is equivalent to giving the audience a visual pause. As you know, if you pause during your presentation, it creates more drama and meaning and reinforces what you have to say.

Going to black gives the audience time to contemplate. Similarly, turning off the projector during a critical part of your presentation allows the audience to feel like they are interacting solely with you, which can build credibility and trust.

The healthiest relationship to have with your slides is one of interdependence. But it's not just about you and your slides finding this balance. There is a third person in this relationship too—the audience.

How do you know when you and your slides show a healthy interdependence? Simply, your slides and your delivery are all about the audience. Instead of using the media to showcase yourself and your dependencies, the audience should be able to see what you're saying. If they feel like they've been enlightened, moved to act, or pushed to change their behavior, then you've been successful.

Nancy Duarte is the founder and CEO of Duarte (www.duarte.com), a leader in developing business presentations for some of the world's most admired companies. Duarte worked closely with Al Gore to develop the presentation that became the Academy Award–winning documentary *An Inconvenient Truth*.

• • •

POWERPOINT SLIDE DESIGN FOR THE ARTISTICALLY CHALLENGED
Ellen Finkelstein

WHEN I ASK AUDIENCES and my subscribers which part of creating a presentation is the hardest for them, the majority invariably say "design." Presenting is so important these days and everyone has to do it. But not everyone has an artistic eye. As you've no doubt noticed as an audience member, there is a lot of substandard presentation design out there.

Why Design Is Important

If you are presenting to potential clients, the press, or the public, you are representing your organization. What kind of impression do you want to give? Most organizations pay professionals to design their websites and printed materials, so why don't PowerPoint presentations receive the same treatment?

In fact, in a sales environment, the presentation is often the point where an organization tries to close a sale—and is thus a crucial step for success.

Moreover, the visual aspect of a presentation is essential for good communication. Images, graphs, and diagrams help the audience understand what you're saying. If they're overly complex, too small, distracting, or unclear, you aren't communicating well.

Can the Rest of Us Design Presentations?

For a high-stakes presentation, I'd recommend using a professional designer. But not all presentations are so critical. Saving money or saving time also are reasons that you may need to design your own presentation.

So how does the artistically challenged presenter create a presentation that looks good and communicates effectively? Because I'm not an artist, yet need to display slides that look good when I write about PowerPoint, I've studied this challenge for a long time. I've read a lot, listened to expert designers, and analyzed slides that I think look good. I've arrived at principles that anyone can use to create a clear, good-looking presentation.

Before you start, keep in mind two overriding principles:

- **Keep it simple.** The simpler your slides, the better they'll look. This is especially true for non-artists, but the great designers also promote simplicity. Simple slides are easier to understand as well.

- **Design for your audience.** Just as you craft your message for your audience, you should design for them. Think how different a presentation for fourth-graders would look from a presentation for college students, accountants, or artists. Overly complex diagrams don't help your audience grasp concepts quickly and don't look appealing either. See the "before" and "after" slides in Figures 4.1 and 4.2.

Figure 4.1.   Before

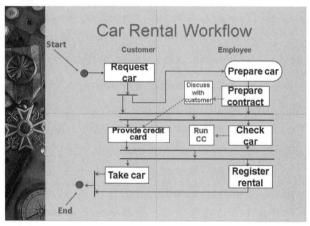

Figure 4.2.   After

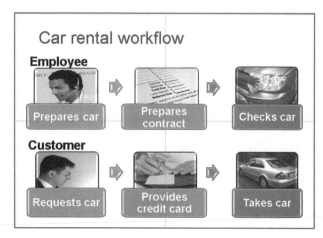

Remove extraneous lines and use images to get instant comprehension from your audience.

Create a Custom Color Scheme

Designers start each presentation by doing something most PowerPoint users never do—they create a custom color scheme. Color schemes can work magic with your presentation because:

- The default colors are dreary and overly familiar.
- Presentation colors should support your branding, including your website and printed brochures.
- Colors should be consistent throughout your presentation. Without a color scheme, you'll often change colors of individual objects on slides. What a waste of time!

To create a custom color scheme, click the Design button on the Formatting toolbar and click "Color Schemes." Click the color scheme closest to what you want and then click Edit Color Schemes. (In PowerPoint 2007, for example, they're called theme colors. On the Design tab, click the Colors button and choose an option. Then click Colors again and choose Create New Theme Colors.)

But the hard part for non-artists is to figure out which colors to use. One secret is to piggyback on the work of artists. Go to your web or print designer and ask for the red-green-blue (RGB) specifications of the colors.

Tip: You can get these colors on your own using the free Colorificator (http://colourificator.sitekit.net/) or another "eyedropper" program that lets you click on a color that you see on the screen and gives you the RGB numbers. For print materials, you'll have to scan them first and then open the resulting image file.

Format the Slide Master

As you probably know, the Slide Master formats the background, specifies font and font treatments, aligns text, and adds images or designs that appear on all slides. The Slide Master can make or break your presentation's look.

It's important to choose a very readable font. Research has shown that sans-serif fonts like Arial, Verdana, and Tahoma are easy to read on-screen, so they're good options. When you pick a font, stick to it throughout the presentation. Use black or dark blue text against a light background and yellow or white text against a dark background.

To avoid having slide titles jump around from slide to slide, do the following:

- Never move the title placeholder on a slide. If the damage is done, display the slide and choose Format > Slide Layout. In the Slide Layout task pane, find the selected layout. Hover the cursor over it, click the down arrow, and choose Reapply Layout. (In PowerPoint 2007, right-click an empty area of the slide and choose Reset Slide.) This simple step can save you hours adjusting individual placeholders.

- Left-justify titles so that they all start at the same place.

- Bottom-justify titles so that one-line and two-line titles always have a common lower-left corner. Double-click the place-holder and choose the Text Box tab. Then set the Text Anchor Point to Bottom. (In 2007, right-click the placeholder and choose Format Shape. Then use the Text Box category and set the Vertical alignment to Bottom.)

Avoid putting your company's logo on the slide master, which puts it on every slide; the audience will quickly tune out and ignore it. Just as you put a logo only on the title page of a report, leave the logo for the title slide and maybe the last slide.

Choose a Background

Top designers today are creating slides with plain white (or black) backgrounds rather than the colorful and elaborate ones we're used to.

The result is a simpler look. White is the new blue in backgrounds, for these reasons:

- Websites usually use a white background and presentation design has followed suit.

- LCD projectors are brighter than they used to be, so you don't have to turn off the lights in most situations. When the lights are on, white isn't as glaring as it once was.

- A plain background enhances the effect of your content and images.

Yet some people want a richer look. You know the backgrounds that come with PowerPoint? Don't use them. People have seen them many times and their use indicates that you don't care very much about creating something new for your audience. Of course, you can easily buy a background; the Internet is full of them.

If you're not an artist, you probably won't be very successful creating an elaborate background from scratch. Instead, try something simple.

Figure 4.3 shows a gray-white gradient using the From Corner shading style.

Figure 4.3.   From Corner Shading Style

The background in Figure 4.4 has a top rectangle of solid blue and a bottom rectangle with a vertical gradient that ranges from 25 percent transparency to 100 percent transparency.

Figure 4.4.   Moving from 25 to 100 Percent Transparency

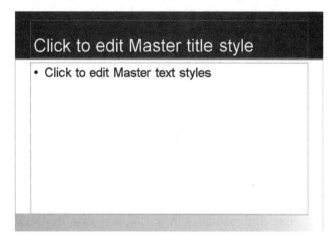

You can place a full-slide photograph on the slide master, as seen in Figure 4.5, or directly on an individual slide.

Figure 4.5.   Photo on Slide Master

Full-slide photos may not play nicely with text. Your text needs to be very clear against the photo. What to do?

- Reduce the contrast and brightness of the photo to create a very pale image. Use the Picture toolbar. (In 2007, use the Format tab > Adjust group.)

- Colorize the photo so that it becomes shades of one color. To do so, change the photo to grayscale (again on the Picture toolbar) and cover it with a semi-transparent rectangle of the color you want. (In 2007, use the Format tab > Adjust group > Recolor button.)

- Use semi-transparent text placeholders, as shown in the full-slide image in Figure 4.5.

- Use the full photo only on the title slide and then crop it to a sidebar on the left for the rest of the presentation

Experiment with white and black backgrounds. Liberate yourself from fancy backgrounds.

Figure 4.6.   White Background with Color Image

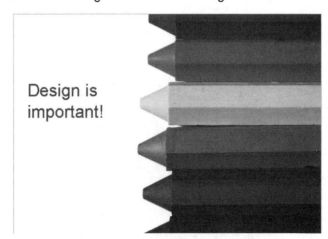

A white background can create a striking slide, like the one in Figure 4.6.

Tell 'n' Show

Tell 'n' show[SM] is my term for slide design that uses a slide title to clearly tell the audience the slide's message, and then uses an image, diagram, or chart to show what you're saying. You tell it, then you show it, just one point per slide. Cliff Atkinson, Michael Alley, and other presentation design consultants have recommended this type of slide design.

When you want your audience to understand and remember what you're saying (and when don't you?), tell 'n' show will help.

Figure 4.7.   Child's Storybook

A child's storybook, as in Figure 4.7, first tells the story, then shows it.

To turn a standard, text-heavy slide into a tell 'n' show slide, rewrite the title so that it actually says something. For example, change "4th Quarter Sales" to "4th Quarter Sales Up 5 Percent." Then add a graphic that shows what you're saying. In this case, it would probably be a graph.

To turn an entire presentation into a tell 'n' show presentation, follow these steps:

1. If a slide makes more than one point, break it up into several slides, one point per slide.

2. Express each point in the title placeholder.

3. Delete all of the bulleted text in the presentation.

4. For each slide, add some type of graphic.

Take a presentation that is mostly bulleted text, do a tell 'n' show makeover, and you'll be amazed at the result. No more death by PowerPoint.

Use photos, not clip art (line art), except in rare cases where you want an iconic effect. If you add a photo with a solid (usually white) background to part of the slide, make the background transparent.

Use the Set Transparent Color button on the Picture toolbar and click the background. (In PowerPoint 2007, choose the Picture Tools Format tab > Adjust group > Recolor drop-down list > Set Transparent Color.)

Use Simple Layouts

Non-artists have a great deal of trouble laying out a slide in an appealing manner. Designers use a grid to help them. If this seems too complex for you, here are some other suggestions:

- Look at magazine ads, billboards, and brochures for layout ideas, find a couple that you like, and use them.

- Keep it simple. An easy layout is a half-slide vertical photo. Crop the photo as necessary and vertically center the text next to it. This layout always looks good.

Renovate Your Old House . . . uh, Presentations

All of these techniques are feasible for non-artists. Take your text-heavy, bullet-heavy slides and redo them using the principles in this article. You'll see a striking improvement and your audiences will appreciate the results, too.

Ellen Finkelstein (www.ellenfinkelstein.com) is a noted presentation design consultant and trainer, a PowerPoint Most Valuable Professional (MVP), and a multi-published author in the presentations field.

• • •

TAKE THE "THREE-WORD CHALLENGE" TO TEST YOUR BULLET-POINT STRENGTH
Rick Altman

WHAT IF A LAW were passed prohibiting bullet points on slides from exceeding three words in length? Could you abide by it? Perhaps not, but humor me on this one, because it stands as one of the best exercises you can do, whether you are the presenter, the content creator, or both. The value of this is so high thanks to two universal axioms for presentation professionals:

1. If a slide contains complete sentences, it is practically impossible for even the most accomplished presenters to avoid reading them word for word.

2. And when you read your slides word for word, you sound like an idiot.

Exhibit One

Here is a classic culprit (Figure 4.8), taken straight from my client files—in this case, a major pharmaceutical company. Somebody simply did an idea dump right into his or her slides, and anyone who tries to speak to this slide is doomed to become a drone and guaranteed to turn the audience members into zombies.

The fourth bullet on the slide is quite different from the first three, suggesting that it shouldn't be a bullet at all. But set that aside for the moment—before you read on, I want you to clean up this slide by mentally reducing each bullet point down to three

Figure 4.8. Classic "Idea Dump" Slide

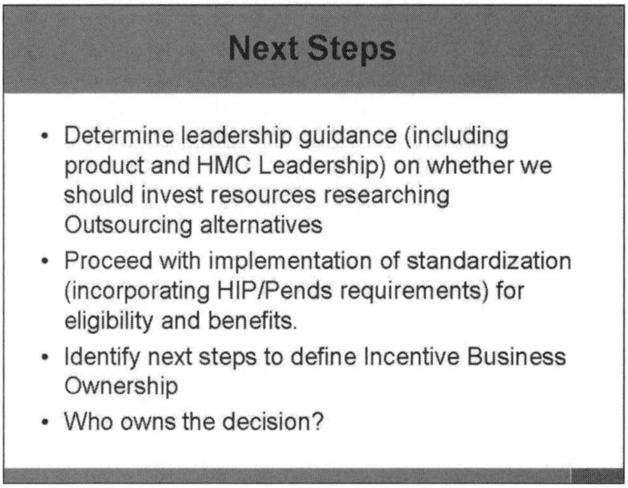

Next Steps

- Determine leadership guidance (including product and HMC Leadership) on whether we should invest resources researching Outsourcing alternatives
- Proceed with implementation of standardization (incorporating HIP/Pends requirements) for eligibility and benefits.
- Identify next steps to define Incentive Business Ownership
- Who owns the decision?

words. Ditch the adjectives, jettison the pronouns, eliminate the flotsam.

Even with your sharpest knife, you might not be able to cut all the way down to three words, but the reward is in the effort.

Figure 4.9 shows my attempt at what I refer to as the Three-Word Challenge.

Figure 4.9. Results of the Three-Word Challenge

Next Steps

- Research outsourcing alternatives
- Standardize incentives for eligibility and benefits
- Define incentive business ownership
- Who owns the decision?

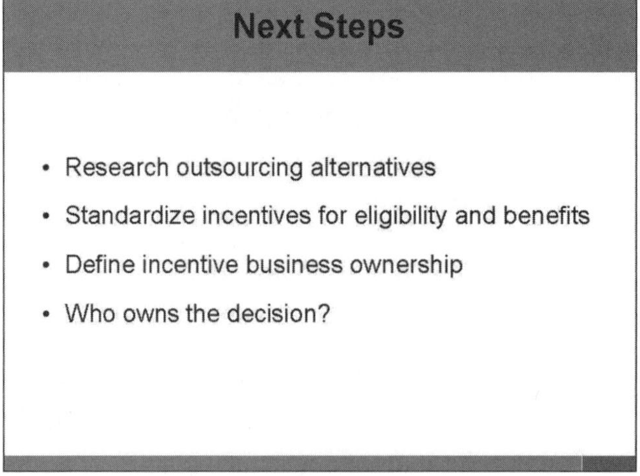

You can see that I failed to get within three words in most cases, but the result of my losing effort is an unqualified victory. The slide is much stronger now, and even though I have no familiarity with the subject, having gone through this process, I feel as if I could almost present on it now.

Benefits of the Three-Word Challenge

Several important things take place when you make an earnest attempt to get within three words:

Your slides are friendlier. With just that one task, you create slides that are much easier on the eyes of your audience. Eye fatigue is the silent killer of presentations. When you ask your audience to sit in a dimly lit room for thirty to sixty minutes, their eyes are going to be the first to go. The more words each slide contains, the quicker the onset of fatigue. Fewer words, less fatigue. Your bullets might not be as descriptive, but that's OK—it's your job to do the describing.

Your pace improves. Something almost magical happens when you reduce the number of words on a slide. Everything seems snappier. The slide draws more quickly, audience members absorb the information more efficiently, and you most likely project more energy.

You create intrigue. In three words, you are not going to be able to fully explain your points. But that's not bad; it's good. In fact, it's terrific! Without having to ask them, you invite audience members to use their imaginations. Once you are good at the three-word rule, you will become a better writer of bullets. You will begin to write with color and humor; you could become coy, even mysterious.

These literary techniques serve to command attention. They help to engage your audience on an emotional level. And that, dear reader, is the holy grail of presenting.

You learn your material better. Of the many bad things associated with dumping complete sentences onto slides, perhaps the

worst is how lazy it makes the presenter, whether it is you or someone for whom you create slides.

Excess verbiage sends a subtle but powerful message that you
don't need to prepare as much, because everything you want to say
is already there. Parsing the words increases your burden as a presenter, but once again, this is a noble burden. Adhering to the three-
word rule forces you to learn your content at a level you otherwise
might not have reached.

One of my favorite quotes about presenting comes from Mark
Twain:

> "If you want me to speak for an hour, I am ready today. If
> you want me to speak for just a few minutes, it will take me
> a few weeks to prepare."

The three-word challenge is a microcosm of the wonderful
dynamic that Twain articulated. In order to get down to three
words, you really need to study the text. You need to truly understand what you intend to communicate and you need to pick three
words that create the perfect backdrop for your ideas. Going down
to three words requires that you practically become intimate with
your text.

While the second of these two slides is certainly a better place
for your audience to be in than the first, the most significant point to
make is the potential that the second slide creates.

Now, perhaps for the first time ever, you, the content creator,
have an opportunity to think like a *slide designer.* With all of that
flotsam on the slide, what chance did you have previously to create
an attractive slide? How could you be evocative? How could you stir
emotion? You couldn't!

But now you have a canvas; you have white space. And it doesn't
require an advanced degree in visual communications to find a stock
photo or company image that might support your message.

In this particular exercise, it took my pharma clients barely half
an hour to reach this point. (See Figure 4.10.)

Figure 4.10.   Sample Pharma Client Slide

Slide Creation as a New Experience

In our workshop that day, we had already discussed the value of creating semi-transparent shapes to better blend imagery with text and this was a perfect opportunity to use that technique: the text lower-left in the slide is in a rounded rectangle, filled black with 50 percent transparency, allowing the photo to show through but still ensuring good contrast.

You only see one rounded corner because the rectangle is hanging over the edge of the slide. Margin controls on the shape ensure that the text appears centered in the visible space.

There is also the question of the fourth point, the "Who owns the decision?" question. Changing it to italic and separating it with a simple white rule serves to reinforce its role as the summarizer of the ideas. Having eliminated the bullet character from these bullets helps, too.

This slide becomes a completely different experience for everyone involved in the equation—the content creator, the presenter, and the audience member. The content creator thinks creatively (perhaps for the first time); the brevity of the text allows the presenter (again, perhaps for the first time) to get out from under the slide and truly communicate directly to the audience; the audience is more likely to feel the weight of the message.

Photos help that cause, just because of the way that our brains receive and process visual information, but the most important part of the equation is the presenter being able to tell a more impactful story, delivered from the burden of all of that text on screen.

Rick Altman is the head of Better Presenting (www.betterpresenting.com), a presentations skills consulting firm in Pleasanton, California, and host of the Presentation Summit, an annual conference for presentation professionals.

• • •

THE POWER OF HIDING SLIDES IN POWERPOINT
Robert Lane

WHEN YOU "HIDE" a slide in PowerPoint, it doesn't display while scrolling through the presentation in Slide Show mode. Why in the world would you ever want to do that—have slides in your deck that the audience can't see? In this article we'll look at several reasons that can greatly increase your flexibility and effectiveness as a speaker, giving talks a more personalized, conversational, audience-friendly feel.

To set the stage, let's consider a common PowerPoint slide. It contains a lot of information—packed from top to bottom with topics to be discussed. A presenter normally walks through point after point, slide after slide until reaching final conclusion slides. Well, that happens in a perfect world, anyway. All too often, our talks don't go quite that smoothly. We start running out of time partway through and desperately wish some of those bullet points, or even entire slides, like the one in Figure 4.11, could be skipped along the way to reach more important content.

Figure 4.11. Sample Slide

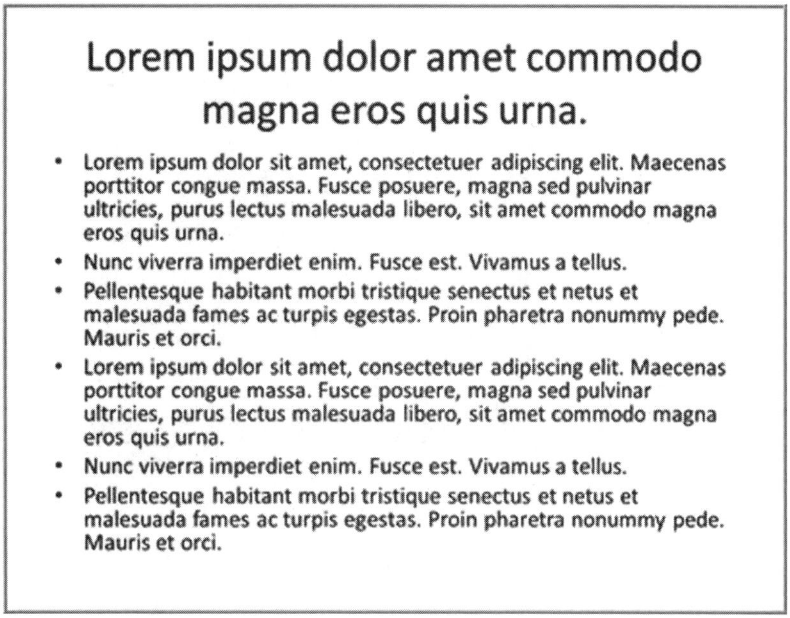

> ### Lorem ipsum dolor amet commodo magna eros quis urna.
>
> - Lorem ipsum dolor sit amet, consectetuer adipiscing elit. Maecenas porttitor congue massa. Fusce posuere, magna sed pulvinar ultricies, purus lectus malesuada libero, sit amet commodo magna eros quis urna.
> - Nunc viverra imperdiet enim. Fusce est. Vivamus a tellus.
> - Pellentesque habitant morbi tristique senectus et netus et malesuada fames ac turpis egestas. Proin pharetra nonummy pede. Mauris et orci.
> - Lorem ipsum dolor sit amet, consectetuer adipiscing elit. Maecenas porttitor congue massa. Fusce posuere, magna sed pulvinar ultricies, purus lectus malesuada libero, sit amet commodo magna eros quis urna.
> - Nunc viverra imperdiet enim. Fusce est. Vivamus a tellus.
> - Pellentesque habitant morbi tristique senectus et netus et malesuada fames ac turpis egestas. Proin pharetra nonummy pede. Mauris et orci.

Maybe you've been in situations as I have in which unexpected circumstances cut your speaking slot in half. Many of us also find ourselves facing uncertainty, realizing along the way that some of the carefully planned agenda is not relevant to our viewers—especially common in sales contexts.

In all cases, wouldn't it be great to have a fast, easy way of making adjustments? Actually, you have that power at your fingertips right now, even with a standard PowerPoint deck. This is where hidden slides become your best friend. Here's how.

Earlier I mentioned that a hidden slide doesn't display when normally scrolling through a show, but it DOES display if accessed via hyperlink. In other words, you can create a simple summary slide like the one shown in Figure 4.12 that links to additional detail on subsequent hidden slides (Figure 4.13).

The presenter then has the option of displaying any amount of extra detail desired, or skipping that detail altogether with a normal

Figure 4.12.   Sample Summary Slide

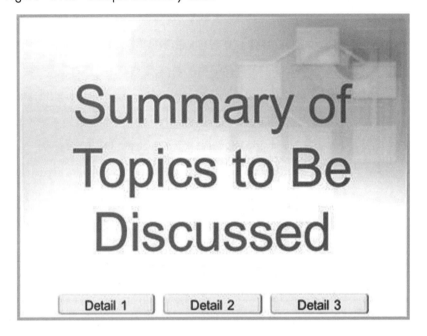

Figure 4.13.   Extra Detail on Subsequent Hidden Slides

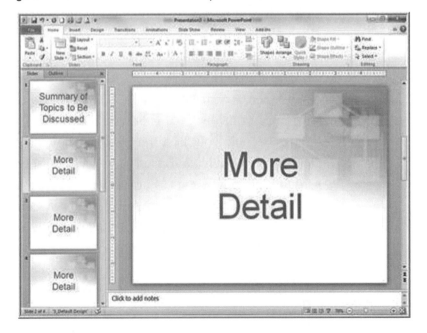

scroll. Entire topics can be nestled away like this and shown only if, and when, needed. This gives you enormous flexibility to adjust timing and relevance in an instant.

For example, try these ideas. Use hidden slides for on-demand display of:

- A full research reference (in large type) if someone asks for the source of your information

- Example pictures that help explain difficult concepts or add information to what you say verbally

- Detailed specs that normally wouldn't be shown but that come in handy for answering specific audience questions or concerns

- Optional charts, diagrams, or tables

- Client-specific slides that only certain individuals or groups are allowed to see

- Audio, video, or embedded documents that you pull up and play/show only if time and audience interest allow

You might even load a show with far more topics than will be needed during a particular talk and have that content in reserve, just in case. Then it's easy to pick and choose what viewers see, customizing a message on-the-fly.

Want to try it? The steps below walk you through building a simple hidden-slide presentation, using techniques that can be easily adapted to your own materials.

Hidden Slides Tutorial

Create a slide show containing four slides. Leave the first slide white, but format the backgrounds of the remaining slides to be red, blue, and yellow respectively by right clicking each slide thumbnail, choosing *Format Background* from the options, and changing background colors accordingly (Figure 4.14). We're doing this simply to tell the slides apart.

Figure 4.14.   Hide the Red and Blue Slides

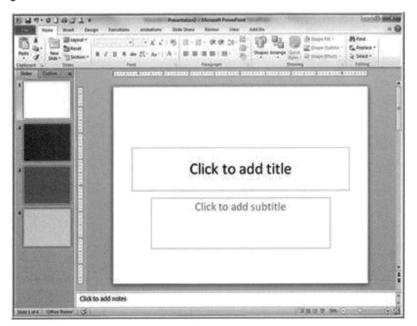

Let's hide the red and blue slides, Slides 2 and 3. Do so by selecting the slide thumbnails and then clicking the *Hide Slide* button on the Ribbon's *Slide Show* tab (PowerPoint 2007 and 2010), or right-click the selected slide thumbnails and choose Hide Slide from the options (Figure 4.15).

When a slide is hidden, its slide number displays with a dashed line and the slide thumbnail displays lighter (PowerPoint 2010 and PowerPoint 2007), as in Figure 4.16. At any time, you can unhide a slide by repeating the steps just described.

Next, click the Slide 1 thumbnail to select Slide 1. Let's start the slide show and scroll to see what happens. Notice that PowerPoint skips the red and blue slides entirely and immediately displays the yellow slide instead.

Now we'll add the hyperlinks. End the slide show and activate Slide 1. Using the *Insert* menu, insert a shape onto its slide pane. Change the fill color of this shape to be red (we will link it to the

Figure 4.15. Two Methods for Hiding Slides

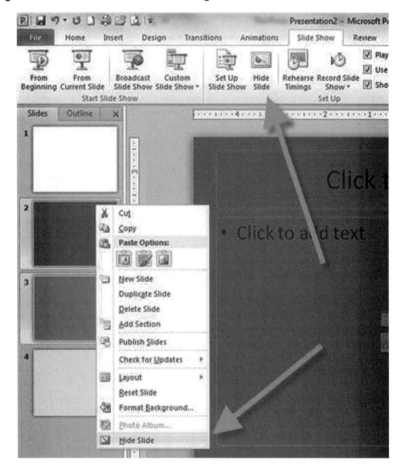

red slide). Add a similar shape beside it and leave its fill color blue (we will link it to the blue slide). Right-click the red shape and choose *Hyperlink* from the options.

Next, click the *Place in This Document* tab so that the four slides available in this show are listed under *Select a place in this document*.

Click the Slide 2 name and then click *OK* to close the dialog box (Figure 4.17). Great! You just linked the red shape on Slide 1 to the

Figure 4.16.   Slide Thumbnails 2 and 3 Display with a Line When Hidden

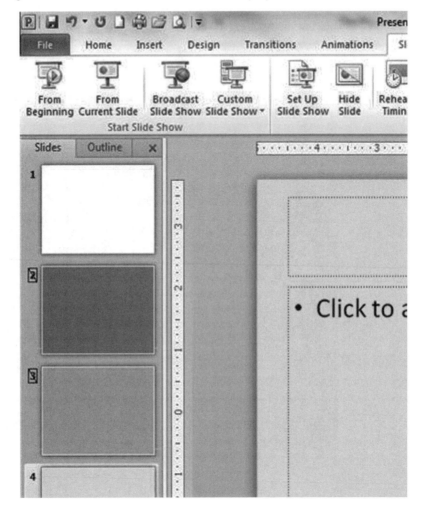

hidden red slide (Slide 2). Do the same with the blue shape, linking it to Slide 3, the hidden blue slide.

Let's see what happens now when running the slide show. Go back to Slide 1 and start the show. Keep in mind that hyperlinks only work while the slide show is running. Click the red shape. The red slide should display immediately. If it doesn't, go back and make

Figure 4.17.   Hyperlinking Shapes on Slide 1 to the Hidden Slides

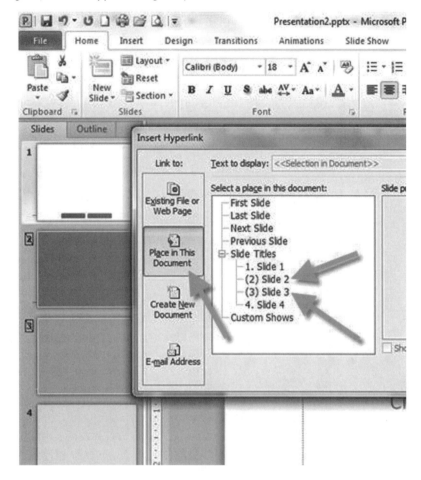

sure your hyperlink is properly in place. Now scroll through the show as normal. Notice PowerPoint shows the blue slide next, as it is the next hidden slide in the presentation. Once you click a hidden slide, the remaining hidden slides will display.

We're almost finished, but let's add one more classy touch to improve these hidden slide techniques. Go to the red slide and add a new shape, and then change the shape fill color to white. We're going to give this shape a special kind of hyperlink called an Action Setting.

Click the shape to make sure it is selected and then click the *Insert* tab on the Ribbon. Next, click the *Action* button. In the *Action Settings* dialog box that appears, select the *Hyperlink to* option and, from its drop-down menu, select *Last Slide Viewed*. Then click *OK*. The result shows in Figure 4.18.

Figure 4.18.   Adding the Last Slide Viewed Action Setting

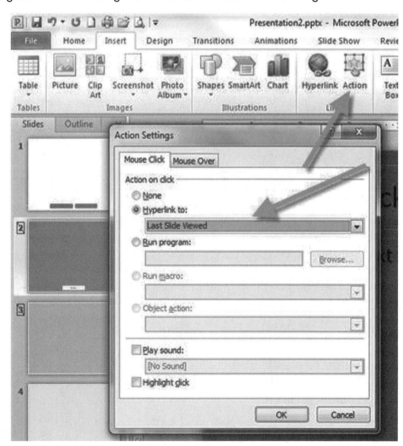

Clicking this shape during a slide show returns you to whatever slide you were on when accessing the red slide in the first place.

In other words, you potentially could add fifty more slides to this show and put a link to the red slide on all fifty slides. In that case, during the performance you might click the red slide link while on Slide 32.

When finished viewing the slide, clicking the red slide's Last Slide Viewed link returns you to Slide 32 automatically. It's a graceful way of jumping out to show extra detail at any time and then returning exactly to where you left off in your presentation track.

Copy the new white shape and paste it onto the blue slide as well. Now you can start the slide show from the beginning and access either the red slide or the blue slide, and then return to the white slide to select another option or scroll to continue with the rest of your talk as usual.

Apply these same techniques now to your own slide shows. Here's an important suggestion. You'll gain even more flexibility and control if you spread topic details across multiple slides, rather than packing them all onto single slides. Having separate pieces of information lets you jump to those points individually.

Robert Lane is the head of Aspire Communications (www.aspirecommunications .com), a Tucson, Arizona–based presentations consulting firm specializing in visually interactive communication practices.

•   •   •

THE LUNACY OF THE LEAVE BEHIND
Rick Altman

I AM A PRAGMATIC BEING. At my core, I understand the values of efficiency and expedience. I embrace the art of compromise and understand that life often gets in the way of ideals and theories. Reality is often harsh, and not adjusting to it often harsher.

Yet, there is one principle relevant to our community on which I do not yield. One ideal to which I hold stubbornly. At this windmill, I gladly tilt. It is the notion that a presentation content creator can create one set of slides that will function ably for the projected content and for the printed material.

This is an impossible notion. Everything else in life might be possible if you work hard, but not this one thing. In my fifteen-plus years as a presentation consultant, I have not once seen it done successfully. *Not once.*

When you set forth to create content for a presentation, you work with two forces that are fundamentally at odds with one another. You want to create projected content that is compelling, and you want to provide information that is useful. The pragmatic being in you usually prevails and, in the interest of time, you look for a happy medium.

Unfortunately, that twain shall not meet. Nary.

As discomfiting as it may be for content creators, a properly prepared set of visuals for a presentation will fail as leave-behind collateral. Your slides are *supposed* to be incomplete; they are supposed to be no more than the tease for the words that you will speak. If they say too much, they inhibit your ability to tell the story.

My colleague and friend Dave Paradi conducts an annual survey of the most annoying qualities of a PowerPoint presentation. The latest survey lists the following as its top three:

1. Speaker reads the slides to the audience

2. Speaker creates full sentences instead of bullet points

3. Text is too small to read

All three of these annoyances are inevitable when content creators attempt to have their slides double as printouts. In other words, this one issue might be responsible for ALL THREE of the sins that have been voted most egregious.

And I'll go one step further: Over-laden slides that try to tell too much turn otherwise smart people into blithering idiots.

Can PowerPoint make you stupid? When there is too much blather being projected, the answer is most decidedly yes.

It is practically a litmus test that we all must take. *How are your visuals? Would they make really lousy printouts? Yes? Great, you're all set to go!*

We live in a world of compromises, but this is one place where you cannot succumb to the expedient route. You must think of your projected content and your printed content as two distinct projects. Otherwise, they both might fail, and you will fail.

A perfect example of this dynamic came to us recently during our ongoing invitation to see work from the presentation community. The Saudi Iron and Steel Company (fictitious company) created a short slide deck on the all-important topic of tire safety. There is probably a lot that you do not know about tire maintenance; I learned several things from surveying a few slides in this deck. Any soccer mom or softball dad would be heavily emotionally invested in this topic.

But when Figure 4.19 arrives on screen, is it going to have an impact? Of course not. And when the well-intentioned presenter begins to speak, it will be almost impossible to avoid reciting the slide. And before you know it . . . instant death by PowerPoint.

Figure 4.19.   Sample Slide with Too Much Text

Tire Safety

Studies of tire safety show that maintaining proper tire pressure, observing tire and vehicle load limits, and inspecting tires for cuts, slashes, and other irregularities are the most important things you can do to avoid tire failure, such as tread separation or blowout and flat tires. These actions, along with other care and maintenance activities, can also:

- Improve vehicle handling
- Help protect you and others from avoidable breakdowns
  and accidents
- Improve fuel economy
- Increase the life of your tires.

Set aside the dubious design motif used here. The real crime committed was when the creator tried to have it both ways and create a presentation deck that could double as printouts.

Figure 4.20 shows the continued decline in what could have been a noble effort: educating an audience about the different qualities of tires and how understanding them would make your car safer.

Figure 4.20.   Additional Examples

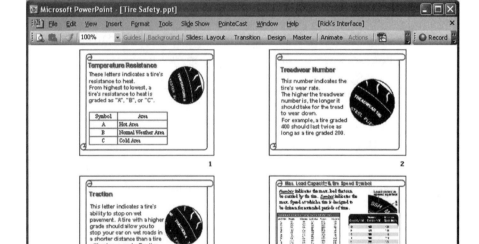

All of these words make it impossible for a presenter to get to where he or she really needs to be: appealing to the emotional side of a story and helping the audience to feel its weight. Very few audience members are moved to action by what their brains tell them; *there must be an emotional component to the story.* Tire safety is low-lying fruit to any parent of a young child who needs to be driven hither and yon to this play date and that gymnastics class.

My makeover of this deck attempts to make the emotional case, while allowing the presenter to inform the audience on the important specifications of tires.

As you can see in Figure 4.21, if these slides were printed and delivered, they would not be very helpful. They require more complete leave-behind information.

Figure 4.21. Slide with an Emotional Component

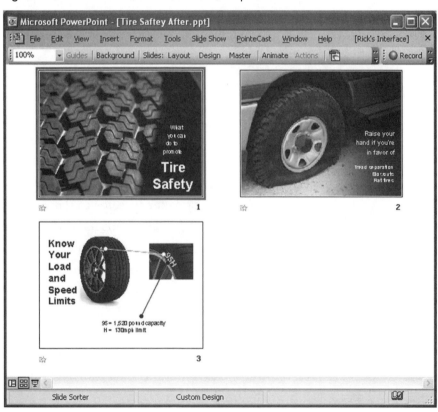

Here are a few ideas and techniques to help you deal with the unavoidable fact that you will need to prepare your material twice—once for the presentation and once for printouts.

1. Acknowledge It Early

The best time to prepare the detail for handouts is before you go anywhere near PowerPoint. Taking notes . . . composing your thoughts . . . fleshing out your ideas . . . these are all great things to do long before you think about how you might engage your audience on multiple levels.

When you prepare the meat of your presentation first, you are more likely to pick a better tool for the printouts, such as a publishing application or a word processor with a good design template. And having pored over the details to this degree, you are in a better position to then choose more compelling visuals to help you tell your audience the story.

2. Use Notes View

If you or your boss committed the popular sin of writing out an entire speech on the slides themselves, you are just one cut-and-paste maneuver away from salvation.

That verbiage belongs in the Notes view, but this is not to suggest that it be there for the speaker to refer to. Having complete sentences in your notes is just as dangerous as displaying them on screen—it could turn you into a drone either way.

The idea here is that *your Notes pages become your printouts*, to be delivered to your audience members during or after the presentation. Notes view in PowerPoint has its own master and can be customized far beyond what most users realize.

Figure 4.22 shows the degree to which Notes view can be designed for optimized leave-behind material. The text here is a direct splice from the original slide.

3. Use Version 2007 Slide Masters

The 2007 version of PowerPoint, to use just one example of the software, has some compelling features that might merit a closer look.

Figure 4.22.   Notes View in PowerPoint

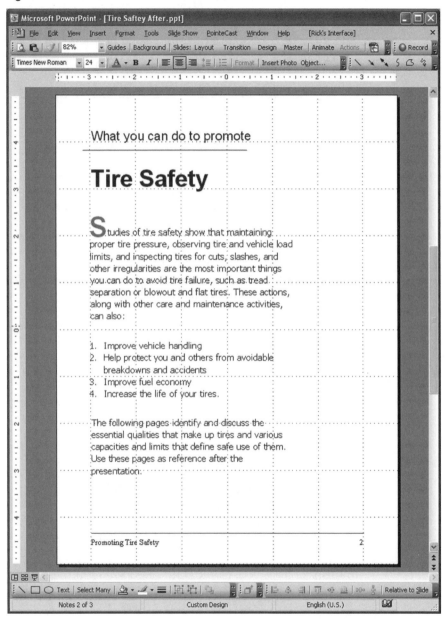

One of them is the flexible layouts that are now part of the slide mastering creation process.

Figure 4.23 shows a layout that is actually rotated 90 degrees, making it optimal for standard printouts. When you apply this layout to a slide, all of the content is rotated to fit a standard portrait layout.

Figure 4.23.   Rotated Layout

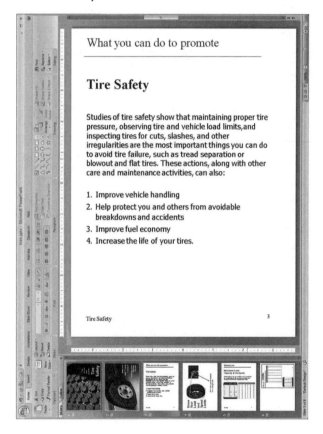

In this scenario, you would either keep hidden the slides that are part of the printouts or create two custom shows, one for display and one for print.

The value of either of these strategies, using Notes view or 2007's slide masters, is your ability to keep the printout material in the presentation file itself, instead of having to deal with two separate files.

But that's the only free lunch here. If you try to cut a corner with leave-behind content, you are guaranteed to fail. If you just suck it up and accept the fact that you need to go the extra mile, your audience will love you for it, and your presentations will be much, much better as a result.

Rick Altman is the head of presentation skills consulting firm Better Presenting (www.betterpresenting.com) in Pleasanton, California, and host of The Presentation Summit conference.

• • •

HONORING ONLINE COPYRIGHT: ONE PICTURE CAN BE WORTH 1,000 HEADACHES
John Billington

HERE ARE FIVE POTENTIAL pitfalls to consider when using images in your PowerPoint presentations. Pictures make presentations work. But the most interesting and compelling images aren't generally found in free clip art galleries. So you comb the Internet, looking for just the right image to convey your message. Click-cut-paste. You've got it!

While you may have "it," that "it" is very likely the copyright-protected work of a photographer or designer. Even for department presentations, sales presentations, training materials, and other internal business purposes, using images without the proper permission and rights is a serious issue and may constitute a breach of the creator's copyright.

To make sure that you stay on the right side of copyright, keep in mind the following.

1. Free Images Aren't Necessarily Free

There are millions of images out there, free for the Googling. Images are available on web portals; image search sites, such as Google

Images and PicSearch; photo-sharing services like Flickr; and the list goes on.

None of these sources make it easy for you to obtain permission to use an image for business purposes. It's far easier to ignore that little warning: "image may be subject to copyright," and just go ahead and help yourself.

Even if an image is freely available on the web, that actually doesn't mean you can freely use it. Drill down and take a look at the source of a photo, and you will often find that the image's owner wants to know who's interested in using the image and for what purpose.

Many photographers allow you to use their work for non-commercial purposes, but they expect to be compensated if you put that image to commercial use—even if that commercial use is within the walls of your organization. Other photographers may restrict even non-commercial use without express permission.

2. What Happens Within Your Company Doesn't Always Stay Within Your Company

Within seconds of an event or a political gaffe, the news is all over the web. Presentations aren't usually quite that viral, but even presentations intended for a small audience can quickly find wide distribution.

For example: an employee sends an internal presentation to a sales prospect. Or perhaps someone "borrows" a few slides for a presentation he plans to deliver at an upcoming tradeshow. The images used in these presentations—sources long since forgotten—are now being disseminated inside and outside your corporate walls.

Without the proper permission to do this, you can open up a whole can of copyright worms.

3. Sharing Isn't Always the Right Thing to Do

Yes, for the most part mom and your kindergarten teacher were right when they told you that it's nice to share. And in today's collaborative workplace, sharing is critical to many of the functions required to stay competitive in the corporate environment. But most of those enticing images on the Internet are not actually ours to share unless we obtain the appropriate permission.

Thanks to awareness raised by the Napster case and more, most of us understand the issues around sharing music and video. Many people also understand the copyright issues involved with using and distributing published written materials and software.

Yet that same level of awareness doesn't always exist when it comes to using images. To include images in presentations and other company communications, organizations must ensure they have obtained the rights to copy, distribute, and display those images, even if the image is free. Photographers, illustrators, and other rights holders can and do track—by tagging, watermarking, and other technical means—who uses their images.

While it may seem impossible for rights holders to know whether you include unlicensed photos in an internal presentation, once you hit "send" with that presentation attached, it is out of your control—yet still your responsibility.

To protect you and your organization, be sure to confirm that you have permission to use and share images before you hit "send."

4. Not All Licenses Are the Same

Chances are you've visited the popular image source Flickr to search for photos. While you can find some great shots on Flickr, those images are often licensed through a Creative Commons license for non-commercial use.

There are other significant issues to consider when using Flickr images. For example, you have no way of knowing for certain whether the person who holds the Creative Commons license is the person who actually holds the copyright for that image.

Another major issue with both Flickr and stock image services centers around third-party rights, such as model and property releases. Virgin Mobile of Australia learned this the hard way when it downloaded a picture from Flickr and used it in a rather unflattering billboard campaign.

The parents of the subject of the photo, a then-fifteen-year-old girl, sued Virgin Mobile. While the photographer owned the copyright and made it available for use under a Creative Commons license that permitted commercial use, he hadn't obtained either a parental consent release or a model release before making the photo available on Flickr.

Stock image services offer some level of commercial usage rights, which is helpful, but terms and conditions can vary significantly, creating both confusion and higher image prices. The frequency and types of use, formats, audience type, and size are all considered in stock image pricing.

John Billington is a product manager at the Copyright Clearance Center (www .copyright.com), a leader in innovative copyright solutions.

• • •

HOW TO CREATE A SLIDE MASTER (OR TWO) IN POWERPOINT
Ellen Finkelstein

I'VE DISCOVERED THAT MANY presenters don't know how to use PowerPoint's slide master. As a result, they create all sorts of workarounds like putting full-slide images on every slide (which makes for a huge file). This especially becomes difficult when they want more than one background. Let's go through the process of creating a presentation with two backgrounds.

1. If you've saved a "better" theme or template, apply it. In PowerPoint 2003, to pick just one version of the software, click Design on the Formatting toolbar to open the Slide Design task pane. You may need to click Design Templates. Then choose your template.

In PowerPoint 2007/2010, you would probably save a theme. To apply it, click the Design tab and select it from the Themes gallery.

2. Choose a color scheme or theme colors.

3. Press Shift and click the Normal View icon at the lower-left (2003) or lower-right (2007/2010) corner of the screen to go into Slide Master view.

4. In 2003, start by formatting the Title Master if you want it to be different from the Slide Master. Then move on to the Slide Master. If you're using 2007 or 2010, click the larger layout thumbnail—it looks like the Title and Content layout—if you want your changes to apply to all layouts. Otherwise, apply changes to the layouts individually.

5. Make the changes you want to the background. You can right-click and choose Format Background or insert content on the Slide Master.

6. To create a second slide master in PowerPoint 2003, choose *Insert > New Slide Master.* If you don't get a Title Master, with the new Slide Master selected in the left pane, choose *Insert > New Title Master.*

To create a second slide master in PowerPoint 2007/2010, from the Slide Master tab (which appears only when you are in Slide Master view), in the Edit Master group, choose Insert Slide Master. You'll see a new, full set of layouts in the left pane. You can choose a new color scheme/theme colors for the second Slide Master if you want.

7. I like to get rid of clutter, so I recommend deleting layouts that you won't use in PowerPoint 2007/2010. Right-click a layout and choose Delete Layout.

8. Repeat the process of designing your template or theme for the second Slide Master.

If you like the result, you might want to save it for future use with these steps:

- Return to Normal view by clicking the Normal View icon.

- In PowerPoint 2003, choose File > Save As. From the Save as Type drop-down list, choose Design Template (*.pot). Usually, this puts you in the "official" Templates folder automatically. Then name the template and click Save.

- In PowerPoint 2007 and 2010, click the Design tab and expand the Themes Gallery. At the bottom, click Save Current Theme. Again, you should be in the "official" Document Themes folder. Name the theme and click Save.

See Step 1 for instructions on using your new template or theme for future presentations. To access both Slide Masters:

- In PowerPoint 2003, open the Slide Design task pane, where you can choose either of the Slide Masters for any slide. Select the slide, click the down arrow next to the Slide Master that you want, and choose Apply to Selected Slides.

- In PowerPoint 2007 and 2010, you'll see both Slide Masters in the Design Gallery, so you can easily choose which one you want for any individual slide. Select the slide, right-click the theme in the Design Gallery, and choose Apply to Selected Slides.

Ellen Finkelstein (www.ellenfinkelstein.com) is a noted presentations skill consultant and trainer, a PowerPoint MVP, and a multi-published author in the presentations field.

• • •

THE MOST VALUABLE POWERPOINT FEATURE YOU'RE NOT USING
Rick Altman

THE BEST-KEPT SECRET OF modern versions of PowerPoint? That's a no-brainer, as I experience it almost every time I interact with users. When I am brought into an organization to consult on presentation skills, most in the room don't know about it. When I give webinars, I can practically hear their "ooh's" and "aah's" when I show it.

I refer to the Selection and Visibility (S&V) Pane, introduced in PowerPoint 2007 and largely overlooked by most users of 2007 and 2010. I attribute this to two things: (1) this function doesn't actually create anything and (2) with lower-resolution displays, the icon shrinks to the size of a pinhead and most don't even see it.

Let's reverse this discouraging trend right now, shall we? The S&V task pane addresses several of the most frustrating aspects of the software over the last decade. It deserves your undying love and devotion. Here are three big reasons why.

Select Objects on a Crowded Slide

The simplest virtue of S&V is the ease it affords you in selecting objects that are hard to reach with a mouse or even invisible to you. When objects overlap one another, reaching the ones on the bottom of the pile has traditionally required contortions, such as temporarily cutting or moving the ones on top or pressing Tab until you think the selection handles maybe kinda, sorta are around the desired object.

Those headaches are all in your rearview mirror now, as Figure 4.24 shows.

With S&V, you can select objects by clicking on their names in the task pane, bringing much-needed sanity to what should be a menial task. Once selected, you can do anything to an object that you otherwise would have. As I said earlier, this pane doesn't really do anything except make it easier for you to do what you want.

Rename Objects

Figure 4.24 might look unusual to you because you had never laid eyes on S&V before, but there is another cause for a raised eyebrow: Circle in the front? Circle in the back? Where did those names come from? Most of you know what kind of names PowerPoint assigns to objects because you have been scratching your heads over them for the better part of a decade:

Rectangle 23

TextBox 9

AutoShape 34

Figure 4.24.   Selecting an Object

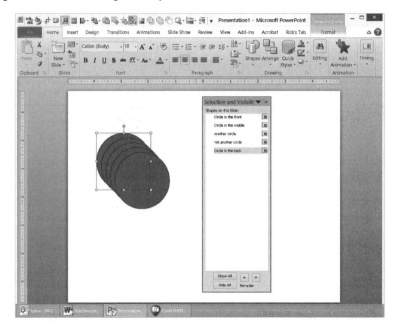

Historically, PowerPoint has been maddeningly obtuse in its naming scheme and you've never been able to do anything about it except curse. But with S&V, you can assign names to your objects that actually make sense. You'd probably do better than "Circle in the Middle," and that's the point: you get to decide what to call your objects.

Renaming objects becomes more than just a cute screenshot opportunity when you have complex animation to create. PowerPoint's obtuse object names are duplicated in the Animation task pane and with ambitious animation needs, you could find yourself drowning in a sea of obtusity.

With Rectangle 23, 24, and 25, which one enters first, which one moves to the center of the slide, and which one fades away? Arrghh!

Thanks to S&V, you can do much better. You can name objects according to their appearance or purpose and have a much easier time creating animations for them.

Case in Point: Solavie, the skin care product that offers formulations for six different earthly environments. To highlight these formulations, the six icons in the lower-right corner move and morph into the six photos across the top, after which each string of text cascades in. So lots of identical shapes doing similar things, one after the other—imagine pulling that off with typical PowerPoint names.

But Figure 4.25 shows how powerful object renaming can be. Each object is named according to its environment type, making the animation process orders of magnitude easier.

Figure 4.25. Object Renaming

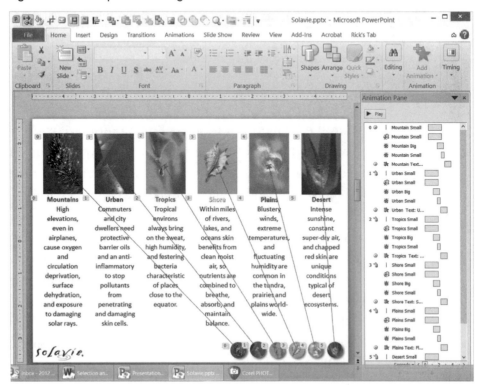

Hide and Unhide

Sometimes it is not enough to be able to name objects. Sometimes you just have to get them the heck out of the way. When you are working on the final parts of a forty-five-second animation, it becomes incredibly tedious to have to start from the beginning each time you want to test it. You need to be able to start from the middle or near the end.

Prior to S&V, if you wanted to temporarily remove an object, you had to cut objects to the Clipboard and work quickly before you accidentally sent something else there. Or work up some bizarre strategy of duplicating a slide, doing your business there, then moving those objects back to the original slide.

Now we have an elegant and simple solution: *make an object invisible*. Figure 4.26 shows the beauty and the genius of hiding objects, as the tail end of the Solavie animation gets the attention that it deserves. As you can see, when you hide an object, it leaves the animation stream, making late-stage testing a piece of cake. Here just the final two environment types are still visible. The earlier four are still there, just temporarily hidden.

Access

S&V lives on the Home ribbon in the Editing group. PowerPoint ribbons have a bad habit of changing right when you might want something on them, and that contributes to the anonymity of a small icon that is there one minute and gone the next.

Indeed, there is no way to predict when you might want to use S&V. Creating, inserting, designing, animating—using S&V cuts across all contexts of PowerPoint operation. So it's helpful to know about its keyboard shortcut of *Alt+F10*. There's no mnemonic that you can apply to that shortcut—it's as easy to forget as the function it belongs to.

You will just have to commit it to memory. When you're in the throes of creation, just press Alt+F10. Pretty good chance that little task pane will come in handy.

Figure 4.26.   Making Objects Invisible

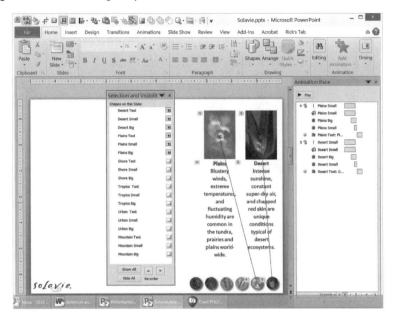

Rick Altman is the head of presentation skills consulting firm Better Presenting (www.betterpresenting.com) in Pleasanton, California, and host of The Presentation Summit conference.

• • •

STAND OUT BY USING VISUAL ALTERNATIVES TO POWERPOINT
Angela DeFinis

WHEN IT COMES TO visual aids for a presentation, what's the first thing you think of? If you said "PowerPoint" or "slideware," you're in the majority. That's the default most presenters rely on. But the answers about visual aids that I've been receiving from my clients recently (and what I've seen at their locations) have surprised even me.

For example, I was working with a client this summer and walked into the training room to find a chalkboard and box of chalk greeting me.

A few weeks later I walked into a client's conference room to find an overhead projector.

Last week I was walking down the halls of a large tech company and peered into a conference room. I saw two walls of whiteboard covered with neatly drawn flow charts, bullet charts, and various other schematics—in bright colors.

A few days ago I was working with a client who used colorful 3×5 index cards to organize his key points and deliver his presentation. He rarely uses slideware but relies instead on his conversational style and deep subject knowledge.

And just yesterday I watched a presentation during which the presenter used a flip chart.

Thriving Without PowerPoint

So when was the last time you used a chalkboard, a whiteboard, a flip chart, or even no visuals at all?

These clients I visited from various industries and organizations—a dental school, a utility company, a software company, a transportation company, and a non-profit organization—all taught me a lesson.

It's easy to become complacent and narrow-minded about the types of visual aids we use—or don't use. It's also easy to fall into the trap of thinking that, to be effective, a visual must be cutting-edge and show off the latest visual gymnastics that PowerPoint can produce.

While I was at each location to share "best practices" and reveal the top design tips and staging usage, I learned that these places and people were effective and had an impact because they knew their audience and used visual tools that they could relate to.

So when it comes to visual aid selection, here's my best advice: Analyze your audience so you know what they expect and what will work for them. Then understand the options available to you. Know what you are comfortable with and what will help you do your best to meet your audience's expectations.

When you follow that guidance, you'll be able to produce visual aids that help both you and your message come alive and connect to the heart and mind of every audience member.

Angela DeFinis is the founder and president of DeFinis Communications (www .definiscommunications.com), a presentation skills training company that offers professional public speaking programs for Fortune 1,000 companies.

5

Graphics Design for the Non-Graphics Professional

Most regular users of PowerPoint or other presentation design software are far from graphic design experts; their expertise usually rests instead in sales or marketing, training, corporate communications, or other disciplines. While many can use PowerPoint's default settings to create basic graphics, those functions aren't always conducive to building the most appealing bar graphs and pie charts or for incorporating Excel spreadsheet data in visually compelling ways.

The tips and advice in this chapter will help the busy non-graphic design professional become more proficient at creating compelling presentation graphics in shorter time frames. Happy designing.

• • •

CREATE SIMPLER, MORE EASILY UNDERSTOOD CHARTS AND GRAPHS
Geetesh Bajaj

THE SIGNIFICANCE OF ANY chart lies in its ability to visually represent complex data as a trend that audiences can easily grasp. So if you create a complex chart with too much detail, you ironically might be creating confusion out of simplicity—even if you aren't aware you are doing it.

One of the easiest ways to make your charts look simpler and less intimidating is by using fewer major units in the "Y" axis—and if that sounds like something that's difficult to understand, then stop worrying and start following these easy steps. This tutorial is targeted to PowerPoint 2007 but will also work in PowerPoint 2010.

Follow these simple steps to change the major unit of Y axis in PowerPoint 2007 or 2010.

1. Select the chart within PowerPoint slide, as shown in Figure 5.1.

Figure 5.1. Chart Editing Mode

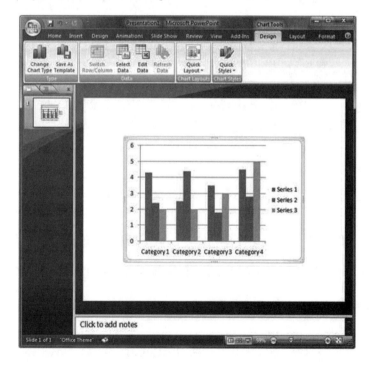

2. Now click on the Vertical Value Axis (the vertical line toward the left of the plot area), as shown in Figure 5.2.

Figure 5.2.   Vertical Value Axis

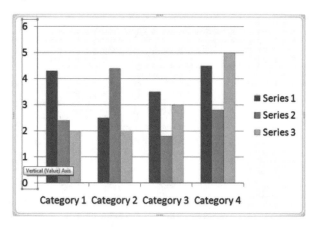

3. Activate the Chart Tools Layout tab of the Ribbon. Toward
    the extreme left of the Ribbon tab, make sure that you have
    selected the Vertical Value Axis—then click the Format Selec-
    tion button (see Figure 5.3).

Figure 5.3.   Format Selection

4. This summons the Format Axis dialog box (as shown in
    Figure 5.4). Select the Axis Options tab from the left pane,
    and you'll find the options explained below in the right pane
    of the dialog box.

Within the Axis Options tab of the dialog box, you'll find these
options:

  • **Minimum:** Set the minimum value for the axis.

Figure 5.4.   Format Axis Options

- **Maximum:** Set maximum value for the axis.

- **Major unit:** Change to display largest increments.

- **Minor unit:** Change to display smallest increments.

- **Values in Reverse Order:** Display the largest value at the bottom of the axis and the smallest at the top.

- **Logarithmic Scale:** Displays the values in a logarithmic, rather than an arithmetic relationship.

- **Display units:** Choose from hundreds, thousands, millions, billions, and trillions. You can also set this as None.

- **Major tick mark type:** Select to define the appearance of tick marks on the specified axis. You can choose between outside, inside, and cross.

- **Minor tick mark type:** This option allows you to set intervals of minor tick marks on the specified axis.

- **Axis labels:** Here you can place the axis label to: next to axis (default), high, or low. Horizontal axis crosses:

  - **Automatic:** This option if selected follows the default setting.

  - **Axis value:** Here you can set the axis cross value.

  - **Maximum axis value:** This option takes the highest value and applies the changes.

5. Now choose the Fixed radio button in Major Unit, and enter the value in the text box, such as 4 (see Figure 5.5).

Figure 5.5.   Major Unit Value

Note: Choose the Major unit value based on the highest value you have for the Vertical Value Axis.

6. When finished, click Close to get back to the chart.

7. Figure 5.6 shows that the Y-axis major unit values now show a difference of 4 points. This makes the chart look cleaner and gives it more visual breathing space.

Figure 5.6.   Y-Axis Values

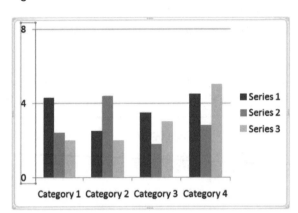

8. Save your presentation, and you now have a simpler, cleaner, more easily grasped chart.

Geetesh Bajaj is the head of Indezine (www.indezine.com), a presentation design studio and content development organization based in Hyderabad, India. He has been designing and training with PowerPoint for fifteen years and is a Microsoft PowerPoint Most Valuable Professional (MVP).

• • •

FOUR WAYS TO TRANSFORM DISORGANIZED GRAPHICS INTO INFLUENTIAL ART
Mike Parkinson

IN THIS ARTICLE I look at a vital, but often overlooked step when creating presentation graphics: *organization and order.*

Have you seen this slide (Figure 5.7)?

Figure 5.7.   Sample of a Complex Presentation Slide

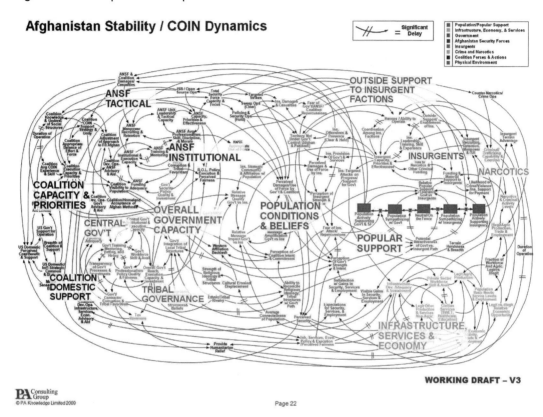

The slide accompanied *The New York Times* article titled, "We Have Met the Enemy and He Is PowerPoint" by Elisabeth Bumiller (www.nytimes.com/2010/04/27/world/27powerpoint.html).

Part of a presentation to Gen. Stanley A. McChrystal and other officials, this graphic depicts the complexity of the American military strategy in Afghanistan. However, if the author of the slide intended to show how the strategy is convoluted and confusing, he succeeded, because no one in the room could follow it.

After viewing this PowerPoint slide, the general commented, *"When we understand that slide, we'll have won the war."*

The graphic is a prime example of "what not to do" when conceptualizing and creating a visual. Although I can find many flaws in this slide, the main issue is a lack of organization and order. Where does the graphic begin? Where does it end? Does this show relationships or a process? Is one element more important than the others?

The author did not follow organization and order "best practices" and created a graphic that is difficult to follow and understand. The result was a presentation that cost the speaker valuable credibility.

The Value of Chunking

As you conceptualize your graphics, "chunk" your information and then assemble the parts into a digestible format, you are using a process I call the *Assembly Method.* Determine the most important bits of information you want to communicate and arrange them to show the relationship between the different elements.

You can chunk information into bullets, shapes, or place them inside of appropriate imagery (pyramids, puzzles, etc.), as shown in the conversion in Figure 5.8.

Figure 5.8.   Pulling Out Primary Topics

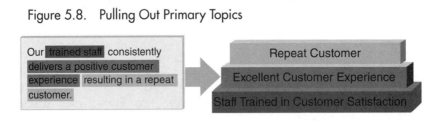

When chunking your graphics, consider how you can assemble the information using *organization, hierarchy, grouping*, and *arrangement* techniques. This step will help you determine what graphic type to use and will make it easier to create a clean, focused, easy-to-follow graphic.

Below are examples of organization and order best practices and how to properly apply them when using the Assembly Method.

1. Organization

There are five major ways to organize information: alphabetical/ sequential, time, magnitude, category, and location (Figure 5.9).

Figure 5.9. Ways to Organize Information

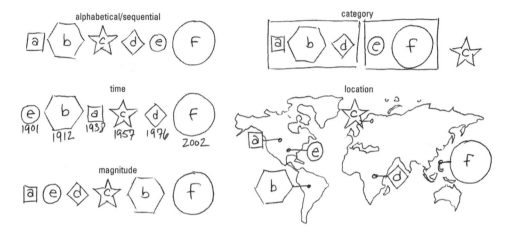

2. Hierarchy

Use color, shade, and positioning to illustrate hierarchy, as in Figure 5.10. Color and shade choices must be made relative to surrounding colors (bright colors dominate only if background colors do not compete for dominance) and graphic flow (left to right versus right to left) is culturally dependent.

3. Grouping

There are three ways to group elements: using a similar physical appearance, organized positioning, and constraining or linking lines or shapes, seen in Figure 5.11.

4. Arrangement

Use a grid to align your lines, shapes, and imagery to ensure your graphic appears ordered and is easy to follow, as in Figure 5.12.

Figure 5.10.   Illustrations of Hierarchy

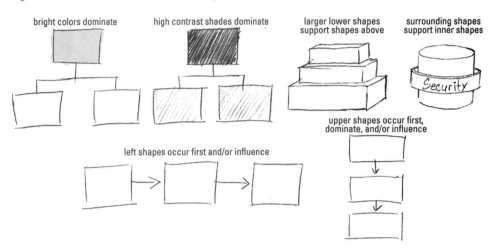

Spotlight is what matters most when chunking. Show only the integral elements, ideas, groups, teams, process steps, or positions. If you need to show greater detail, consider breaking the graphic into different visuals. Make an overview graphic (using it as a roadmap to your details) and highlight key parts with blowouts revealing greater detail on subsequent slides.

Figure 5.11.   Grouping Elements

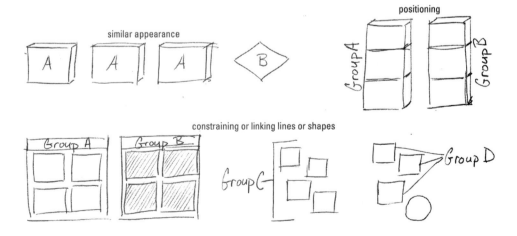

Figure 5.12.   Grid Arrangement

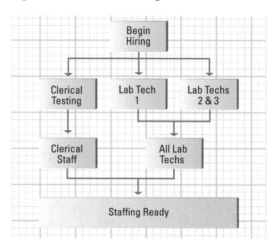

Organization and order forces you to think through the messages you want to share. Follow these rules and your graphic will be clear and communicative and your audience will understand your slide— no small feat in today's presentations world.

Mike Parkinson is the CEO of Billion Dollar Graphics (www.billiondollargraphics .com) and is an internationally recognized visual communication expert and multi-published author.

• • •

HOW TO INSERT SMARTART GRAPHICS IN POWERPOINT
Geetesh Bajaj

SMARTART IS A component within PowerPoint 2007 and 2010 for Windows that replaces the diagram options in previous versions of PowerPoint. SmartArt also allows you to replace bullet points with infographic content using text-within-shapes that's more logical to view and present.

I'm going to walk you through how to insert SmartArt graphics within PowerPoint 2010:

1. Create a new presentation, or open an existing presentation in PowerPoint.

2. When you insert a new slide in PowerPoint, it uses the default Title and Content Slide layout. But if you open a new presentation, it opens a new slide with the default Title Slide layout, which you have to change to Title and Content.

3. Click the Layout button/option in the Home tab of the ribbon to bring up the Layout gallery, as shown in Figure 5.13. Select any of the layouts that include a content placeholder (the small palette-like collection of multicolored buttons visible on some of the slide layouts (see Figure 5.13 again).

Figure 5.13. Choose a Slide Layout That Includes a Content Placeholder

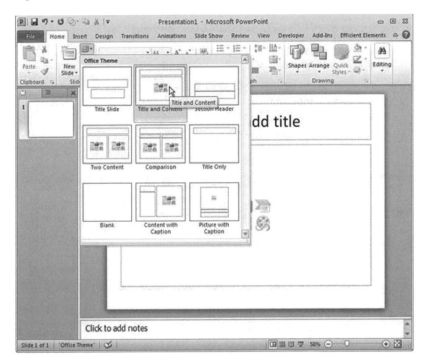

4. If your slide layout has a content placeholder, click the *Insert SmartArt Graphic* button among the six buttons in the content placeholder that you can see in the slide within Figure 5.14.

Figure 5.14. Content Placeholder

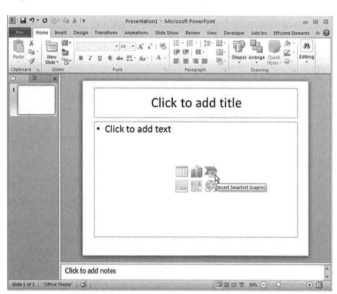

Alternatively, if you want to insert a SmartArt in an existing slide that has no content placeholder, just select the Insert tab of the ribbon, and click the SmartArt button, as shown in Figure 5.15.

Figure 5.15. SmartArt Button

5. Either of these options opens the Choose a SmartArt Graphic dialog box that you can see in Figure 5.16.

Figure 5.16.   SmartArt Dialog Box Options

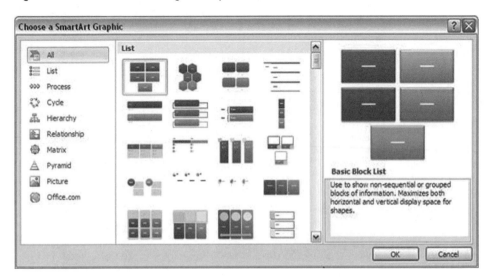

The left pane lists the types of SmartArt graphics available, the middle area displays SmartArt graphic variants within the selected type, and the area toward the right shows a preview of the selected SmartArt graphic, along with a brief description.

6. Select any of the SmartArt graphic variants you want to insert, and click OK.

7. This will place the selected SmartArt graphic on the slide, as shown in Figure 5.17.

Figure 5.17.　SmartArt Graphic on Slide

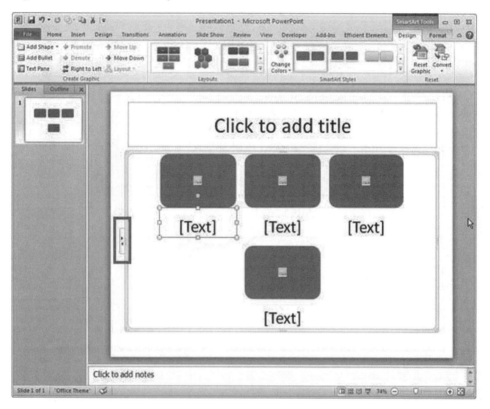

8. When the SmartArt graphic is placed on the slide, click the arrows located on the left side (highlighted in Figure 5.17) to open the text pane (see Figure 5.18).

9. Any text content added or edited within the text pane shows up within the SmartArt graphic as well.

10. Save your presentation, and you are finished.

Geetesh Bajaj is the head of Indezine (www.indezine.com), a presentation design studio and content development organization based in Hyderabad, India. He also is a PowerPoint Most Valuable Professional (MVP).

Figure 5.18. SmartArt Graphic Text Pane

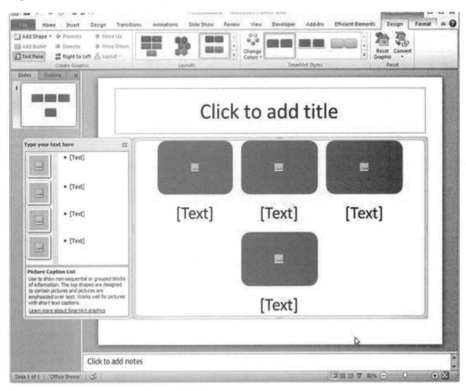

• • •

HOW TO USE EXCEL MORE EFFECTIVELY IN POWERPOINT
Dave Paradi

EXCEL IS COMMONLY used to perform calculations or financial analyses. I use it frequently for these purposes, as I am sure you do. While Excel is a great tool for performing numeric analysis, it is not intended to be a presentation device. If you show a large spreadsheet on the screen, people become overwhelmed quickly and tune out.

But there are ways around that. I'm going to share some best practices for using the information from an Excel analysis in a presentation. In the first part, I'll demonstrate how to use a table of numbers from the spreadsheet on a slide. In the second part, I'll cover ways to use the data in ways other than the "copy and paste" approach that most presenters favor.

Part 1: Summary Tables

If you shouldn't just copy and paste the entire spreadsheet on a slide, what should you do instead? Create a *summary table.*

Any analysis we do should answer a question that prompted the analysis. How are this year's results compared to last year? How are results compared to our forecast? What do projections show for the next three quarters? What factors contributed to the rise or fall in results?

Your audience does not want, or need, to see all of the analysis. They only need to see the results that answer the question. So create a summary of the results from your analysis in Excel. It could be on a portion of the existing worksheet or on a new worksheet. This summary table is what you'll use on your slide. It should be a few rows by a few columns at most. This makes it easy to understand and large enough when displayed on the screen.

When you copy this small number of cells to your slide, I suggest you use one of four options. PowerPoint allows more, but I think these are the four that are most useful to consider.

I've listed the options below, along with an idea of what the result will be in your slide. Three of the four are accessed by using the *Paste Special* command, which opens up a dialog box that gives you more options than the default Paste command.

Option 1: Simple Paste Using Ctrl + V, Which Inserts Your Excel Cells as a PowerPoint Table

PowerPoint tables can only be animated as "all on" or "all off," so you can't build the rows or columns individually unless you use the exit animation reveal technique. This option does not link to the source Excel file, so any changes in the Excel file will not be reflected in your presentation automatically.

Option 2: Paste Special; Excel Worksheet Object

This option embeds the current version of the Excel worksheet into your PowerPoint slide and displays the last editing view of the worksheet. The advantage to this method is that it allows you to access the entire sheet on your slide.

The disadvantage is that the last view is shown, so someone can accidentally open the object and what shows up on your slide will be what that person last looked at, perhaps not what you wanted the audience to see. This method also uses the limited table animation and does not link to the source Excel file.

Option 3: Paste Special; Unformatted Text

This option creates a PowerPoint text box of the entries in the cells, using tabs to create the columns in the text box. Because it is a text box, you have more control over formatting the text and you can animate it like any other text box, including by row. There is no link to the source data.

Option 4: Paste Link; Excel Worksheet Object

This option embeds a link to the Excel file on your slide and displays the last view in Excel. When you edit this object on your slide, it actually opens Excel to do the editing. For animation, it treats it as a single object, so you only have the "all on" or "all off" options.

This link does update your slide as data in the Excel sheet changes (you will be asked to update the data when you open the PowerPoint file). This option is great if you have a regularly updated spreadsheet and only want to create one presentation that will always have the latest data.

None of these options is the best in all situations. Consider the purpose and future use of the summary table of numbers, then select which option works best for you.

Part 2: Creating Visuals Instead of Tables of Data

While showing a table of numbers is one option for presenting data calculated in Excel, it is not the only one, nor is it the best option in many cases. Here I want to explain other best practices you can use to present numerical information from Excel.

If you are showing a trend in some data or comparing a few figures, use a graph in PowerPoint instead of a table of numbers. If you show a table of numbers and expect your audience to do the math to figure out the difference in magnitude between the numbers, they won't. Audiences don't want to do math you should have already calculated. Instead, use a graph to illustrate the differences in the numbers.

Don't feel that you have to re-type the data and risk making a mistake. Just copy and paste the data from Excel to the PowerPoint graph data table.

I rarely suggest showing a full table of numbers, but if you must show such a table, make sure it is not overwhelming for your audience. There are two techniques you can use to make a table easier to understand.

First, if the table is small, use a callout to focus attention on the one or two numbers that are the most important. Put a circle around the number and add some text beside it to explain why the number is significant.

If the table is large, and you need to explain each area separately, use the break-down and zoom-in technique. Start by showing the entire table for context, but explain that there are different regions of the table that you will explain in detail and show the regions by semi-transparent overlays on the large table. This gives the audience an overall context for the organization of the data and how the different regions relate to each other.

Then you can show a zoomed-in portion of the table to explain each region individually, using the callout technique to focus attention on the one or two numbers in that region that are most important.

The final best practice is one that allows you to build audience input into the calculations. This makes it very personal to their circumstance and raises the level of audience engagement. This technique can work well when you have calculated a general example in Excel and show the results to illustrate a broad concept.

The idea is communicated, but the applicability to an individual situation might not be clear. In this case, hyperlink to a pre-created Excel spreadsheet that allows you to ask the audience for input. Let the spreadsheet do the calculations using their input, giving results that are tailored to their exact situation.

This engages the audience and demonstrates your point using input that exactly matches their situation, the kind of involvement audiences usually appreciate.

You also now have an example you can e-mail participants right after the presentation that demonstrates their exact scenarios, reinforcing the message delivered in the presentation.

Just because you use Excel to calculate data for use in a presentation doesn't mean you have to copy and paste a large table of intimidating data onto a slide. Use these techniques to present a more visual message that communicates more effectively with your audience.

Dave Paradi runs the Think Outside the Slide website (www.thinkoutsidetheslide .com), is a consultant on high-stakes presentations, the author of seven books, and is a PowerPoint Most Valuable Professional (MVP).

• • •

WORKING WITH GRAPHS CREATED OUTSIDE OF POWERPOINT
Dave Paradi

GRAPHS THAT YOU CREATE in PowerPoint are easy to work with and present because you can animate them easily. But not all of our graphs will be created in PowerPoint. Sometimes we will need to use a graph that has been created in a graphics program and saved as an image file, posted on a website, or included in a PDF file. You may also deal with technical graphs that are output to image files from special software programs.

We don't want to, or cannot, re-create these graphs in PowerPoint, so how do we present them effectively?

The main problem you face when presenting graphs is that you can't animate them. They are static images and can't be broken into series of data like graphs created in PowerPoint.

With a PowerPoint graph, you can build it piece by piece to explain the data one piece at a time. A graph image cannot be built piece by piece. And since many of these graphs are complex, building them piece by piece would help the audience understand the visual much better.

One of my slide makeover videos showed an example of this challenge. The graph is a complex water analysis graph and it was hard to see the patterns of the data. Without seeing the trend, the message of the visual was lost. And since the source data were not available, it was impossible to re-create the slide using PowerPoint's graphing feature.

People followed up with me after that video and asked how I had done the makeover. Let me explain, since it provides some good lessons for dealing with these graph image situations.

Figures 5.19 and 5.20 show the "before" and "after" slides from the makeover.

First, I decided on the most important point the graph was making. In the case of the makeover graph, it was about showing a decline in the measured value over time. In your case it may be a trend line that shows financial data or it might be one of the lines already on a graph that you want to highlight as the key focus of the data.

Second, I placed the graph image on the slide and made it as large as I could. This may involve cropping out excess room around the graph or cropping out the title of the graph (since the slide title will be the headline). After cropping, I can resize the graph, making sure to hold down the Shift key as I drag a corner handle so the graph keeps the aspect ratio and does not become distorted.

Figure 5.19.   Before Makeover

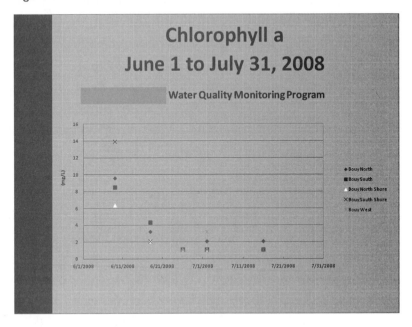

Figure 5.20.   After Makeover

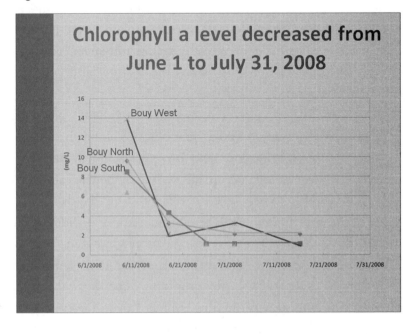

Third, I used the freeform line tool to draw a multi-segmented line through the data points in the graph to show the trend. Depending on your need, it may be a simple straight line or another shape, perhaps a rectangle, to go over a bar or column.

With this shape, I can set the color and thickness so it is easy to see. Drawing on top of the graph is the key to making it easy to understand because it gives you objects in PowerPoint that can be animated.

My final step was to animate the line so it built in the direction I wanted and in the sequence I needed to deliver the message. You will have to determine what order and direction the shapes you have drawn on top of the graph need to build in order to communicate the message you want.

When you're faced with using an image of a graph in PowerPoint, use the steps in this article to make your presentation more effective.

Dave Paradi runs the Think Outside the Slide website (www.thinkoutsidetheslide .com), is a consultant on high-stakes presentations, the author of seven books, and a PowerPoint Most Valuable Professional (MVP).

• • •

PRESENTING FINANCIAL DATA: PUT YOUR NUMBERS ON A DIET
Dave Paradi

YOU ARE A PRESENTER who deals with a lot of numbers. Maybe they are financial results, operational analysis, or market research. You live in Excel and love spreadsheets. So naturally, when you have to present to others, you include almost every number you have. Doesn't everyone love numbers the way you do?

Unfortunately, no.

I'd like to suggest what you should present instead of all the numbers. Let's start with why presenters feel like they have to include all the numbers they've calculated. First, they believe that if they include everything, the audience will better understand what they are trying to say. Unfortunately, the opposite is true.

A slide full of numbers makes most people mentally check out. The second reason presenters include all the numbers is that they feel that they have to show how much work was done. If they don't show a lot of numbers, the audience won't think they worked hard doing the analysis. Trust me, they will be able to tell whether you worked hard or not in ways other than how many numbers are in your presentation.

I believe that presenters have the responsibility to figure out what the numbers mean to the audience and only present that information. It may require a few numbers, but certainly not all the numbers in the analysis.

As a presenter, look for a change between time periods and draw a conclusion on whether that is a positive or negative change. Look at the trend over a longer period of time and determine whether that trend needs to change in order for the organization to succeed. Look at the differences in results between different regions or products to conclude where future efforts should be directed.

Your audience wants to know what the numbers mean to them.

When designing slides to present your analysis, start by writing a headline that summarizes the one point that you want to communicate. If you have more than one key point, create more than one slide. This headline drives what visual you will put on the slide. Sketch the visuals, which may be a small summary table of numbers with indicators to show whether the numbers are good or bad, a graph showing a trend or relative results, or a diagram illustrating results through a process.

Whatever visual you select, it will support the headline that you wrote. And it won't be a slide with a spreadsheet full of numbers.

Most professionals are passionate about their work and have an emotional attachment to it. That is what makes my suggestions even harder to implement. When I suggest only including a few of the numbers or a summary graph, it is natural to have an emotional reaction: "What do you mean I can't show everything I did? Don't you know how much work I put into this?"

I do know how much work you put in. And the audience will see your effort when you provide an insight that makes their decisions and work easier.

In a recent workshop I showed how an organization could take a slide with six hundred numbers on it (I am not exaggerating, I counted) and reduce it to the ten numbers that the executives really needed to know. The improvement in clarity was amazing. You can achieve the same clarity by focusing on what the audience really needs to know.

Dave Paradi runs the Think Outside the Slide website (www.thinkoutsidetheslide
.com), is a consultant on high-stakes presentations, the author of seven books, and
a PowerPoint Most Valuable Professional (MVP).

6

Mastering New Presentation Media

WEBINARS, MOBILE PRESENTING, AND SOCIAL MEDIA

It used to be when you thought of presentations you conjured a speaker standing before an audience projecting PowerPoint slides with a laptop-and-projector setup. But today it's just as common for businesspeople to deliver presentations over the web or using mobile devices like iPad tablets. In addition, more presenters are posting presentations to outlets like YouTube or SlideShare as well as allowing audiences to offer live, in-session feedback using social media tools like Twitter.

Presenting or posting content in these mediums creates new design and delivery challenges. Webinar presenters need different strategies for keeping audiences engaged when they can't see them, for example, and when multi-tasking beckons to participants sitting before computer screens. When presenting with tablets, presenters need new skills such as adapting PowerPoint or other slideware for use in that format.

The use of web conferencing and mobile device presenting only promises to grow, so it's smart to begin developing competencies in these areas now, so you're not caught unprepared when the time comes for you to design or deliver content in these new presentation mediums.

• • •

PRESENTING WITH YOUR IPAD: FIRST QUESTIONS FIRST
Geetesh Bajaj

S O YOU HAVE AN APPLE IPAD and you've been asked to present in front of a small or large audience. Just the thought of delivering that presentation using the iPad rather than your regular laptop and the ubiquitous Microsoft PowerPoint (or Apple Keynote) makes your blood pump faster.

For many of us it may not even matter whether we still use a laptop or a desktop to present. Even if we use the iPad along with a laptop, it will still be an achievement of some proportion. Welcome to the club of so many others thinking exactly like you.

There are two distinct iPad presenting scenarios, and they differ by just one word: presenting *on* an iPad or presenting *from* an iPad.

Presenting *on* an iPad means that you use your iPad to present or share information with one or a small group of people. You need no connected projectors or wireless video signals, and you are happy to use the iPad screen as your display. You often pass the iPad to others in the audience, and they may share their iPads with you, too, if this is a collaborative group presentation.

Your presentation may or may not be based on slideware such as Microsoft PowerPoint or Apple Keynote. In fact you might be sharing content that is from a website, an e-mail message, or just some notes. You may also be typing notes on your iPad as you conduct the presentation.

Many presenters have found this to be a great way to share information within a small group. Of course, this way of presenting also includes those who use PowerPoint or Keynote to present to others using just the iPad, again to a fairly small audience that comprises one or two.

Presenting *from* an iPad is a different animal. It's similar to presenting from a laptop connected to a projector or another external display. It's just that you want to use your iPad as a substitute for the laptop.

People ask a lot of questions about this scenario, ranging from what will happen to their existing PowerPoint or Keynote slides to what sort of multimedia support they can expect on the iPad. Also, how can they open PowerPoint slides at all on their iPads? Finally, does it matter whether they are Windows or Mac users?

Adapting Slides for iPad Presenting

I will answer one of those questions here: How to adapt slides for iPad presenting. One of the many ways in which you can adapt PowerPoint slides to an iPad-friendly format is by converting all your slides to pictures. This approach will work well for slides that have no animation or multimedia—and the good news is that great presentation slides can be created without animation or multimedia of any sort.

The bad news is that this is a one-way street—and if you want to make any changes to your slides, you will have to edit your original presentation and convert the slides again to individual pictures.

Figure 6.1 shows the sixteen-slide presentation I started with—these are all slides from a Photo Album presentation, and each

Figure 6.1.   Pictures in PowerPoint Slide View

slide has a photograph and caption. Your slides may be like more conventional PowerPoint slides, and it does not matter because the process for all types of slides is the same.

To convert your individual slides to pictures in PowerPoint, you summon the Save As dialog box and choose JPG or another graphic format as the file type. The process works the same way to export JPGs in any PowerPoint version on both Windows and Mac. You will ultimately end up with plenty of pictures that are suffixed with their original slide numbers, that is, the first slide in your sixteen-slide presentation will be named Slide1.JPG, and the last slide will be named Slide16.JPG.

Of course, you may not have sixteen slides—that's just the number of slides that I started with, as shown in Figure 6.1.

At this time, it is a good idea to rename your first nine slides so that Slide1.JPG now reads Slide01.JPG (see Figure 6.2).

Figure 6.2.   JPGs in PowerPoint Deck

Thereafter, place these slides in a folder that is indexed by iTunes. To learn more about how iTunes indexes picture folders, simply search the term "add photos to iTunes library" on Google.

Depending on which version of iTunes you are using, or if you use Windows or a Mac, the process may differ. Apple also has a great tutorial called Syncing Photos Using iTunes.

The next time you sync your iPad (both iPad 1 and 2) with your iTunes, the slide pictures will be copied and available within your iPad's Photos app.

Once you have synced your iPad, launch the Photos app on the device to see whether all your slides have been imported as pictures. Also be sure that they are sequenced in the order you want to show them as slides, as shown in Figure 6.3.

Figure 6.3. Photos on the iPad App

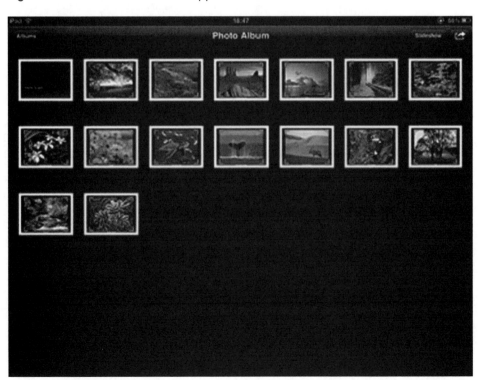

Thereafter, you can show these picture slides from your iPad. Moving on to the next slide is as easy as moving on to the next picture. And since the Photos app is AirPlay available even on iPad 1, you can use it with an Apple TV or even a VGA cable connected to a projector. This may not be the most elegant way to transport your PowerPoint slides to an iPad, but it does work.

Note: Even though Apple's documentation says PNGs are supported by the Photos app on iPad, and by iTunes to sync, I found that iTunes ignored all PNGs—that may be just a fluke, but JPGs do work the best.

Geetesh Bajaj, who heads Indezine (www.indezine.com), a presentation design studio and content development organization based in Hyderabad, India, has been designing and training with PowerPoint for fifteen years and is a Microsoft Power-Point MVP (Most Valuable Professional).

• • •

STRUGGLING WITH WEB-BASED SALES PRESENTATIONS? TRY THESE TIPS
Dave Paradi

IF YOU HAVEN'T BEEN involved in designing and delivering presentations over the web yet, it's an important skill to learn. With more businesses having a global scope and travel budgets still under pressure, more and more sales meetings are being held virtually rather than in person.

Here are a few technology tips to help you avoid potential pitfalls and create smoother, more fruitful sales presentations over the web.

Use a Second PC as a "Participant"

No matter how fast your web connection is or how fast the connection of any participant is, there will always be a slight delay between when you show the next slide and when participants see the slide on their screens. By the time the web conferencing platform takes your new slide, transmits it to the system's server, and then sends it out to each participant, anywhere from one to several seconds will elapse.

The challenge is that you will not know when the participants are seeing the new slide unless you set up a second PC on your desk and connect that PC as a participant. That way, you can advance to the next slide and keep transitioning with what you are saying until you see the new slide on the "participant PC."

Use this step to ensure your words always match the visuals your participants are seeing.

Use a Standard Screen Resolution

Many computers today come with high-resolution monitors that can be quite large. Even laptops have wide screens that can show full HD resolution videos. But in almost all cases, the higher resolution will hurt instead of help your presentation.

The 1680 by 1050 widescreen monitor I am using right now has almost 2.25 times as many pixels as a normal XGA resolution of 1024 by 768 (which is the resolution of most projectors). That means that a web conferencing service will have to send 4.5 times as much data each time (2.25 times from your computer to the server and 2.25 times from the server to the participant).

The upshot is much slower load times for each slide and longer waits for the participants to see the next slide. And if participants don't have a high enough resolution on their screens, your well-designed visual may appear distorted or perhaps not even appear at all.

I suggest reducing the resolution of your screen to 1024 by 768 (or something close) so that slides appear more quickly and look crisp on each participant's screen. You can always change the resolution back after the web conference is over.

Beware Drawing Tools

One feature that many web meeting services highlight is the ability to use drawing tools during your presentation. Most of the services allow the presenter to grab a virtual pen or highlighter and draw on the screen.

While this sounds like a great idea in concept, travel with care. Movement is very hard to show smoothly during web meetings. Too often when you draw, create a circle around an important concept, or highlight a key phrase, it will look jerky to the participants.

This jerkiness makes audiences think that something isn't working properly or they missed something, which distracts from your message. Instead of using the drawing tools, create proper callouts that direct attention to the important spots on your slides.

Don't Restrict Yourself to Slides

Too often presenters think that the only content they can share in webinars is a set of slides. Not true. Within PowerPoint, you can link out to other software programs and provide a seamless transition for your audience.

For example, if you are meeting with a prospect to discuss a problem she needs to solve, one thing you might do is put the financial data she gives you into a spreadsheet to calculate the magnitude of the issue.

Why not hyperlink out to that pre-created spreadsheet from a slide and fill out the numbers right there so she can see the calculation happen before her eyes? The prospect will then be able to clearly see the impact of changing parameters as the figures automatically recalculate.

This also gives you an agreed-on measurement that can be easily included in an e-mail or formal proposal after the meeting is concluded.

As you start to replace more in-person meetings with web meetings, keep these best practices in mind. You'll find the meetings becoming more productive and you'll reach your sales objectives faster.

Dave Paradi runs the Think Outside the Slide website (www.thinkoutsidetheslide .com), is a consultant on high-stakes presentations, the author of seven books, and is a PowerPoint Most Valuable Professional (MVP).

• • •

IS TWITTER A PRESENTER'S DREAM COME TRUE . . . OR A NIGHTMARE?
Cliff Atkinson

FOR A TINY COMPANY that produces tiny messages, Twitter has had an outsize impact on public consciousness. It seems every company, celebrity, and blogger has jumped on the Twitter bandwagon, sending 140-character tweets from every location and on every topic imaginable.

But for a presenter, it seems that tweets and slides are two different tools in two completely different worlds, and never the twain shall meet. But the two worlds actually have been colliding on an epic scale lately, as it becomes more common for audiences to use Twitter during live presentations.

Twitter can be a positive force for improving presentation quality, but its existence should also give pause to presenters trying to get by with less-than-stellar presentations.

Consider these real-life presenter nightmares that have happened in the recent past:

- A keynote presenter is on stage delivering his talk. Unknown to him, audience members start tweeting out to the world about how poorly designed his slides are, how outdated and off-target his content is, and how trapped and powerless they feel in the room. The negative comments build on one another, and by the end of the presentation, someone creates a T-shirt available for sale at a website that reads, "I Survived the Keynote Disaster."

- Another keynote presenter stands at the podium, bright lights shining in her eyes, without the laptop she had expected to be able to use. Unable to comfortably read her notes, she becomes nervous and starts to rush through her material. Audience members start tweeting their comments, which are displayed publicly on stage, noting that she is rushing and they can't understand her.

Although these two experiences were unpleasant for the presenters, they are powerful lessons to all of us that things are changing extremely fast in the field of presentations. Even if no one in your own audiences is using Twitter today during a presentation, as soon as tomorrow they could have Twitter installed on their smart phones, tablets, or laptops and be typing away to thousands of followers.

If you do nothing to prepare for the use of Twitter by your audiences, the consequences could be a nightmare, as in these examples; but if you prepare for the inevitable, you can make sure that Twitter becomes more of a dream come true.

The best way to prepare for your tweeting audience is to make at least four positive assumptions about Twitter and how it can serve both you and them.

1. Assume Your Audience Is Using Twitter to Take Notes and Spread the Good Word About You and Your Ideas

If you have one hundred people in your audience, and they each have one hundred followers, your potential audience for your ideas has just expanded from one hundred people in the room to ten thousand around the world.

As you do the hard work you've always done to deliver an effective presentation, you suddenly have much greater capability to reach more people with no additional work. With this positive view, be sure to make your most important points tweet-able in the form of succinct, quotable statements.

2. Assume Twitter Is a Two-Way Tool You Can Use to Open a Dialog with Your Audience

Like PowerPoint, Twitter is a tool that can be used for good or for bad. To use it for good, open a Twitter account and engage your audience before, during, and after your presentation. Use Twitter beforehand to research your audience and solicit case studies and challenges they face. Use it during the presentation when you take Twitter breaks to answer questions and get a feel for the temperature of the audience. Use Twitter after your talk to follow up on open items and keep the conversation going.

Because you can make a record of all of the tweets your audience has made during your talk, this "Twitterstream" is a goldmine of audience feedback, showing you which of your ideas and techniques were a hit, and which ones were a miss that you can then revise for the next time.

3. Assume Your Audiences Want to Be More Involved Than Ever

If your audience is using Twitter, they're likely online and a few clicks away from finding all the information in the world they need. If your audience can find the details on their own, you can spend less time on the details and instead leave more time for involvement such as exercises, case studies, and practical application of your ideas.

Our new era of social media is leading to more participatory forms of communication that unlock knowledge and learning from within a group of people, which shifts the emphasis for speakers from presentation more toward facilitation.

4. Assume You Remain in Control

Be proactive and welcome the backchannel at the start of your talk. Let them know you may be reading and sharing what they wrote to the whole group during a Twitter break. This simple act removes the feeling of anonymity that backchannel commenters sometimes feel they have and ensures people know that they should only write what they feel comfortable having you read publicly.

Also, be sure to provide an event hashtag—a code followed by the # sign that Twitter users include in posts about your talk. By including it in your marketing material and on your title slide, along with your Twitter username, you visibly demonstrate you are ready to fully engage the backchannel.

Although there are bound to be more road bumps as audiences and speakers work out the new dynamics that Twitter introduces to presentations, it will continue to remain the case that people grant the floor to speakers to guide an experience.

Just as you have been responsible for matching your material to your audience, keeping them engaged and leaving them feeling satisfied, you also are responsible for managing the change when audiences start to tweet. You can manage the change best when you embrace Twitter, and guide it to become the dream come true that it has the potential to be.

Cliff Atkinson is a writer, speaker, and consultant to CEOs who wrote the bestselling book *Beyond Bullet Points* (www.beyondbulletpoints.com). He used his method to create the presentations that helped persuade a jury to award a $253 million verdict to the plaintiff in the nation's first Vioxx trial.

• • •

CONSIDER ALTERNATIVES TO USING VIDEO IN WEB PRESENTATIONS
Dave Paradi

NOT LONG AGO a professional speaking colleague called on me to help her with an upcoming webinar. It was her first significant webinar for clients, and she obviously wanted it to go well. One of the elements she wanted to include in her presentation was a video clip that illustrated some key concepts.

Here is the approach I recommended that will allow you to have the benefit of a video clip without actually showing it during a webinar.

Why not just embed the video on a slide and show it like you do in a live presentation? On all the webinar platforms I've used, using video seems to be among the biggest problems. In my experience, video over the web does not work well when embedded on a PowerPoint slide. It works better when played in a media player outside PowerPoint, but it still suffers from "stutters" due to the limitations of the bandwidth on a live transmission.

The reason watching content such as YouTube or Brainshark slide makeover videos posted to a website works well is that your local computer downloads a portion of the video first so that it plays smoothly from your local computer. Live video in a webinar can't do this.

So how can you get the benefits of using an illustrative video clip in a webinar?

You use a series of screen captures from the video to make your points. Let's start with the planning first. When you are showing any video clip, you're using it to illustrate specific points. You may be showing a demonstration of a technique or process or you may be using a video testimonial to reinforce a claim you've made. There are specific images or words you want to emphasize. Make a list of those specific spots in the video.

Play the video at the highest quality possible and pause it when you reach one of the spots you've made note of in the planning stage. Take a screen capture of that image using *Alt + PrintScreen* and paste the image on a PowerPoint slide. Make the image as large as you can without distorting it too much and crop out the controls of the video player so you are just left with the image.

Once you have the image on the slide, add a callout so the audience knows what they are supposed to look for in the image. It may be an arrow and text to point out something in the image or it could be a specific quote that a person is saying that is reinforced with the expression on her face.

Keep capturing images from the video and creating slides until you have all the spots on your planned list in your presentation. When you are presenting the slides during the webinar, you can introduce the section by saying that you want to show a series of images from a video clip that illustrate the point you were discussing.

You can go through the images fairly rapidly, as quickly as one every eight to ten seconds if necessary. Remember that there is a lag between when you show the next slide and when the audience sees it, so you can't advance through the images as rapidly as you could in a live presentation.

By using a series of screen capture images instead of a video during a web presentation, you increase the quality of the experience for your audience and still use the video to illustrate the points you want to make.

Dave Paradi runs the Think Outside the Slide website (www.thinkoutsidetheslide .com), is a consultant on high-stakes presentations, the author of seven books, and is a PowerPoint Most Valuable Professional (MVP).

• • •

HOW TO POST YOUR PRESENTATION AS A VIDEO TO YOUTUBE
Ellen Finkelstein

I receive plenty of requests for information on how to post a presentation as a video to *YouTube*. Here are four good options to do so:

1. Use PowerPoint 2010. It outputs to WMV format. Use the commands *Choose File > Save and Send > Create a Video*. Then

choose from a couple of options, as you see in Figure 6.4. You can use existing timings for each slide or assign a timing. This is the absolute easiest method. The video output will include sounds and narration, and even embedded videos.

Figure 6.4. Creating a Video

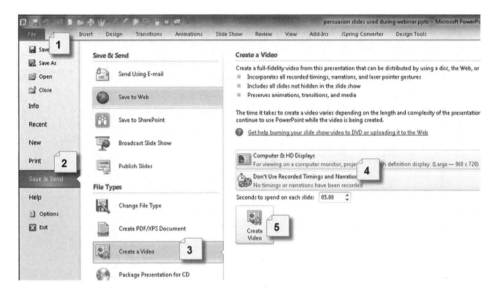

2. Use Techsmith Camtasia Studio. For longer presentations, and when you want editing capabilities, Camtasia is a great tool with lots of features. Camtasia is video-recording software, so you run through your presentation and Camtasia creates a video. You can record your voice as you go. Techsmith's Snagit also can record video, but you won't receive any editing or narration features. Snagit helps you create eye-catching videos for easy sharing.

3. CamStudio is free, open-source video-recording software.

4. Authorstream, a presentation-sharing site, lets you convert up to five minutes to video and upload it to YouTube. They have paid versions that will let you convert more time.

To achieve the best results, you'll need to know about slide timing and perhaps narration. When you have your video output, you simply upload it to YouTube the same way you would upload any other video.

Ellen Finkelstein (www.ellenfinkelstein.com) is a noted presentation design consultant and trainer, a PowerPoint Most Valuable Professional (MVP), and a multi-published author in the presentations field.

7

The Art of Persuasion

HOW INFLUENCE REALLY HAPPENS DURING PRESENTATIONS

The end game for any presentation is *persuasion*, or getting audience members to think or behave differently based on what they've just seen or heard. But plenty of myths exist about how influence really happens, and it's the rare presenter who understands the art and science of persuasion.

Most presenters focus only on selling the upside of their ideas or solutions, for example, when research shows people are generally more persuaded by what they might *lose* than by what they might *gain*. Another school of thought holds that text and data are the best tools for swaying audiences—using facts or figures to change hearts or minds—when in reality making a lasting impact requires appealing more to the right side of audiences' brains, not the left. Influencing the right brain only happens through use of things like powerful personal stories or interactive group discussion.

What makes a presentation memorable is the emotion and stories behind the data. This chapter provides a host of proven, research-based techniques for helping you improve your personal influence as a presenter.

• • •

FACTS JUST AREN'T WHAT THEY USED TO BE
Jim Endicott

PROBABLY ONE OF THE most fundamental, most foundational beliefs around the presentation process is that whoever makes the best case wins the day. Key customers will be compelled to purchase your product or service based on a great datasheet. Partners will be overwhelmed with your command of a spreadsheet and opt-in. And employees will embrace the need for an extended pay freeze because of your compelling presentation of Q3's troubling financials. I have two words for you . . . *not likely.*

Unfortunately, research shows that changing belief systems seems to happen a lot less often than we would like to believe. In a 2008 joint study with Duke University and Georgia State University, researchers set out to understand how effective facts are at swaying opinion. As a study context, they focused on documented misconceptions that prevail today around certain political views. Could blatantly false or unsubstantiated beliefs be corrected with an objective communication of the actual "truth"?

The results in a moment. . . . Although this particular study was politically focused, presenters must embrace the fact we are continually trying to alter belief systems. When I get up in front of a group to deliver a keynote around winning the hearts and minds of busy people, I try to alter the belief system that a good deck of PowerPoint slides is all that is needed to win over an audience.

For you, the issue may be that global warming is a real threat, your software product can address issues that have been plaguing people for decades, or that donating to your local non-profit can really change lives.

Let me net out for you what pages of research revealed: *All information is filtered through an audience's existing belief system.*

When individuals believe something very strongly, the exposure to contradictory information (even if true) can actually reinforce the existing (incorrect) belief system. People will go to great lengths to avoid the cognitive dissonance created when their beliefs don't seem to jive with the facts.

Sorry to rain on your parade, but it would seem that facts and data work best when people already agree with us!

So what does it take to change hearts and minds? In the book *The Leader's Voice* (Clarke & Crossland), the authors studied the personal communication vehicles that leaders used to be highly effective. What they discovered is that there are three compelling "channels" used purposefully and at strategic times to create personal impact. They are (1) factual, (2) emotional, and (3) symbolic.

The factual channel is great to prove, inform, and justify but is weak in actual persuasion and influence. The emotional channel, best characterized by more right-brain influences like personal stories, relational interaction, and visually rich sensory stimulus, is the stuff that motivates and inspires change and can bypass an audience's natural defenses (and belief systems).

The third channel is the symbolic used to align thinking and focus efforts. (For example, have you ever had a manager who gave his or her whole team a physical object that had special meaning for creating a change in thinking?)

Unfortunately, today most presenters camp heavily on the factual channel and wonder why their presentations so often fail to achieve the results they worked so hard for.

You want to know why we teach executives to be better, more compelling storytellers? This is why. This is also why we help sales organizations work to balance a factual, data-driven appeal with a relational (emotional) story of impact or innovation.

Changing what audiences think and believe is not for the faint of heart, and it requires us to be much smarter.

For some, this will make perfect sense. For others, who are convinced their pie charts and tabular data is their secret sauce for closing the deal, I probably won't be changing your minds anytime soon.

Jim Endicott is president of Distinction Communication Inc. (www.distinction-services.com), a Newberg, Oregon, consulting firm specializing in message development, presentation design, and delivery skills coaching.

• • •

PRESENTING TO PERSUADE
Dianna Booher

EVERYBODY IS IN SALES. Your job may be to sell your ideas, training topics, conclusions, budget, strategic vision, products, or services to an audience of two, twenty, or two thousand. Many people consider persuasive presentations to a client or boss the most difficult of all because there is often much at stake in the audience's action or inaction—a commission check, a promotion, a career.

Yet practice in persuasion has been plentiful: Have you ever persuaded a professor to change a grade? A store clerk to give you a refund—against published policy? A traffic cop to let you off with only a warning ticket? A seller to negotiate a discount? A date to go out with you? A teenager to stay in school? A bureaucrat to make an exception?

Consider Your Demeanor

Create flair and drama as you present a new idea, topic, recommendation, product, or service to your audience. Having wanted to shed the huckster image of the stereotypical "salesman," many presenters have gone to the other extreme and removed all animation, inflection, and energy from their delivery style in an effort to come across as more "sincere."

Instead of sincere, the result has been lackluster and boring. If you're not passionate about your topic, neither will your audience be. *Never confuse genuine enthusiasm for lack of professionalism.* If you want to see the power to move a world to action, watch the delivery styles of world leaders and listen to their vocal variety.

Don't let a passionless demeanor destroy your audience's confidence in your offering.

Imagine You Have to Report on Your Success

If your purpose is to instruct a group of employees on taking credit-card applications over the phone, then you can measure whether you achieved that purpose fairly easily: Can they complete the applications without error?

If your purpose is to motivate them to adopt a healthier lifestyle, you can determine your success by the actions they take: increased exercise, reduced stress, more nutritious, healthier meals, and so forth.

Thinking of the pressure of having to measure and report on your specific success—what your audience members do or do not remember, do or do not do, understand or do not understand—will lead you to focus on the essentials of your content.

This focus ultimately helps you to weed out the "nice to include" ideas and information from the "must include" ideas and information—a particularly helpful practice when you know a lot about your topic and have less time than you would like to share it.

Visualize yourself measuring and reporting on your results with your audience, and sort and sift your information accordingly.

Never Let Facts Speak for Themselves

Facts need interpretation. According to Mark Twain, "There are three kinds of lies: lies, damned lies, and statistics." If you don't believe this, take a look at the most recent presidential campaign. People can make facts and numbers mean almost anything. Interpret yours so that your listeners draw the same conclusions you intend.

Add Volume to Increase Authority

In our society, little girls are taught that loud voices are not feminine, while boys learn no such inhibitions. As a result, women often have problems with speaking loudly enough. In today's business arena, wimpy voices receive little attention.

Consider the extreme. When someone shouts, everyone turns to look—regardless of what's being said. Volume captures attention. Volume adds energy to your voice; it has the power to command or lose listeners' attention.

Know When Not to Quote an Expert

Certainly, experts lend authority to your persuasive effort. If you quote the plant manager about the efficiency of the equipment, followed by the engineering operator, and then a leading manufacturing rep in the industry, they may all pile on great data to help you make your point more persuasive.

Similarly, motivating employees to become leaders, think creatively, embrace change, and provide better customer service requires moments of inspiration. One or two pithy quotations can sell an idea and motivate audiences to action.

However, ten or twelve quotations dropped into a presentation can drown any breath of fresh air from the speaker. Avoid quoting so many experts that you diminish your own authority.

Use the Principle of Scarcity

With a gas station on every corner, you do not worry much about a low fuel tank. If the price of gasoline posted on one service station sign looks too high, you drive on down the road to compare prices.

But your behavior changes dramatically when you are about to enter the desert with a less-than-full tank and see a sign that reads: "Last gasoline station for the next 180 miles."

You can use this same principle of scarcity when you are selling ideas. Point out limitations—ideas, time frame, budget, workers—and see whether you increase the impact of your words and speed up decisions.

Identify and Use Meaningful Proof

Many presenters have wasted enormous amounts of time gathering proof of their points—only to discover that their audience did not agree that the studies, surveys, focus-group findings, or work samples proved anything.

Make the proof meaningful to those whose opinions count. For example, you may prove that the new engine from Vendor A is faster than any on the market and will solve all your backlogged welding projects. However, if your executive group says the backlogged welding projects are a minor blip in the overall profitability picture, then all your proof will be beside the point.

Create Immediacy

If you are a single adult reading a news story about a teenager killed on a motorcycle because he wasn't wearing a safety helmet, you may feel sorry, shake your head, and continue reading.

However, if you just bought your eighteen-year-old a motorcycle and had an argument with him or her about the importance of wearing a safety helmet, you probably will tune in a little closer to the statistics to find out how you can convince your son or daughter to wear a helmet.

Bring your presentation issue as close to home as possible. Make your audience see, hear, touch, and feel the situation.

If the members of your management team hear about the low unemployment rate on the news, they will have a general awareness of the difficulty of retaining competent employees. However, if you cite the 38 percent increase in employee turnover at your Detroit plant, adding that the company's rehiring and retraining costs hit the half-million mark for the past year, these managers will quickly see the urgency of the employee-retention problem.

Whether you are talking about money, management, communication, or marital problems, appeal to your listeners emotionally.

Then supply the information to help them justify their decisions logically.

Never Underestimate the "Like" Factor

Have you ever noticed that the grocery sacker begins to talk to you about the weather, sports, or whatever as he or she pushes your grocery cart to your car? Or that the cab driver asks whether you are in town on business or pleasure and where you are from and how your flight was? Or how often the waiter at the restaurant comments on your cute kids?

And then have you noticed how much bigger the tip you give to these service people is than tips to those who are sullen, grumpy, or reserved?

It should come as no surprise that when your audience likes you, they are more likely to be persuaded about what you have to say.

Ask for a Suspension of Judgment

When you know your listeners will likely be biased against what you have to say, admit that situation. Not bluntly, of course, but diplomatically. Chances are good that they will give you a fair hearing.

It's amazing what people will do when you simply acknowledge and ask.

Leave Out Limp Language

Buyers of ideas know to beware when they hear words like these: "This *may* be appropriate in your situation." "I'll *try* to get the survey and report completed by next month." "This diagnostic testing *usually* works." "*Most* of the users in our department find this feature well worth the money."

Limp language says to the audience, "I'm not really sure and do not want to go out on a limb with a definite statement that you can hold me to."

Disclaimers and qualifiers yell "loophole, loophole" in the minds of listeners. Of course, you never state something outright that you cannot support. However, neither should you be in the habit of filling your presentation with disclaimers such as "Guarantees are subject to change without notice" or "Delivery schedules may vary, of course, depending on peak workloads."

Even if you're not in sales, your power to persuade is crucial for your personal and professional success—to get a job, promotion, or raise, to lower your cable bill, or to talk your way out of a traffic ticket. Use these principles to present your case with confidence.

Dianna Booher is the CEO of Booher Consultants (www.booher.com) in Dallas, Texas, and works with organizations to increase their productivity and effectiveness through better oral, written, interpersonal, and cross-functional communication.

• • •

HALLWAYS OF INFLUENCE: MASTERING THE ART OF IMPROMPTU PRESENTATIONS
Patricia Fripp

RECENTLY, I WAS TALKING to a member of a consulting firm who faced a vexing presentations problem. He often found himself struggling to express himself when approached in the hall by the head of another department or a senior executive. For him, it was much easier to speak in front of a large group than to master the skill of the water-cooler vignette.

He believed that larger venues gave him more time for all-important preparation. "The impromptu meetings really catch you off guard," he said.

This was no trivial matter. The man was spearheading a new department at his firm, and he had countless opportunities to use his business acumen to make a lasting impression on colleagues in everyday encounters in hallways or lunchrooms.

He told me he often walks away wondering whether he has left people thinking more about his rambling communication skills than his brilliant ideas. He asked me, "How should I handle these moments more appropriately?"

Here is what I told him:

> "Outside of your home, ALL speaking is public speaking. There is no such thing as private speaking. You're right that many people are more comfortable when they have time to prepare for a speech than when they must communicate off the cuff in more informal settings. But conversations on the elevator or at the water cooler can do as much to boost your career as giving a formal presentation."

So how do you master impromptu meetings and on-the-spot interactions?

Here are five tips:

1. *Focus on others.* The silver bullet in business is the "like" factor. But it's easy to become so caught up in what others are thinking of you that you forget one of the most effective business skills is to express interest in others' lives and work.

Know what is going on in your company or unit so you can congratulate people on their achievements or refer to a previous conversation: "How was that trip you took last week?"

Your sincere interest in people in your orbit will make a lasting impression.

2. *Ask questions to initiate and sustain conversation.* A bright but introverted friend of mine has a gregarious wife who often drags him to parties where he doesn't know anyone. He used to sit in a corner with a drink in his hand, inspecting the carpet. Then I showed him the question-asking technique.

At the next gathering, he asked the hostess about her work. "I'm an emergency room nurse," she said. "What is your average day like?" he responded. They talked for an hour. As the couple prepared to leave, the hostess told my friend's astonished wife, "Your husband is one of the best conversationalists I've ever met."

Moral: When you make people feel important, letting them talk about themselves and sharing what they know, you earn a reputation as a brilliant conversationalist, even if you've hardly said a word.

3. *Have something to say that is of interest and topical.* Keep up with the news, and peruse your corporate report or newsletter regularly. Have two or three relevant things to say at all times. You can even "rehearse" with a trusted friend for those chance encounters with CEOs or other senior leaders.

4. *Praise others.* For example, be sure to boast about your entire team or business unit rather than your own efforts. Say how proud you are of them and offer highlights of their accomplishments. It makes you more likable, and the unavoidable implication is that you are a good leader.

5. *Work to overcome shyness.* When you find yourself in an elevator with a senior leader, forget the power plays and do what would make your mother proud. Be cordial, smile, breathe deeply, and take the initiative. Say, "Good morning Mr./Ms. Big Shot. I don't know if you remember me. I am Patricia Fripp, and I work in the communications department."

Then congratulate the person on a recent success—a speech, quarterly results, published article, award, or new business contract. Or mention very briefly an achievement or improvement in your department: "Did you hear how we saved the company a quarter of a million dollars?"

You have seconds to connect, so don't try to pin Big Shot down. Perhaps Big Shot will stop to continue the chat when you reach your floor, but more likely you've planted the seeds for future conversation.

Patricia Fripp (www.fripp.com) is a San Francisco–based executive speech coach, sales trainer, and award-winning keynote speaker.

● ● ●

AUDIENCE TRUST: IT'S YOURS TO LOSE
Greg Owen-Boger

RECENTLY, I WAS coaching a senior executive on a very high-stakes presentation. He told me he wanted to be perceived as trustworthy. Setting trustworthiness as a goal is common among our clients, so there was nothing new about it in this situation.

But as the discussion went on, he asked me what he could do to ensure that his audience saw him as worthy of its trust.

How to Build Trust

His question had me stumped for a bit. Just what exactly *can* someone do to be perceived as trustworthy? Words won't do it. Saying "trust me" is an engraved invitation NOT to.

You can't stand a certain way, or gesture or smile in a way that would build trust. Presenting solid data is certainly a good and necessary thing to do, but it alone won't build trust.

Then it occurred to me.

"Their trust is yours to lose," I said.

I went on to explain that this particular audience is there because they already trust him. They wouldn't bother if that weren't true.

So rather than thinking about ways to build trust, we should think of ways to maintain the trust we already have. We do that by being truthful, genuine, smart, and attentive to an audience's needs and views.

We do it by looking them in the eye and really seeing them. We do it by creating excellent visual aids with accurate data. We do it by answering their questions and concerns with complete transparency, even when the data isn't in our favor.

Finally, we do it by putting their needs ahead of our own.

And the nice thing is, when we do these things, the trust they already have in us grows.

Greg Owen-Boger is a vice president with Turpin Communication (www .turpincommunication.com), a presentation skills training company in Chicago, Illinois.

8

Winning the Pitch

DELIVERING EFFECTIVE SALES PRESENTATIONS

There are few places where the quality of your presentation skills are so exposed—and where the stakes are higher—as in sales presentations. Convincing prospects to select your products or services over a bevy of global competitors is challenge enough. Couple that with the pressure of having to deliver a well-targeted and flawlessly executed pitch with no technology slipups, and it can be a nerve-wracking scenario.

Delivering winning sales presentations not only requires good technical presenting skills, it also demands that presenters understand human psychology and be able to mind-read prospects. People buy for a variety of reasons, but most do so for a time-honored reason: *because they feel understood, not because they're made to understand.* Understanding that distinction often means the difference between winning the prospect's business and settling for also-ran status.

• • •

THE TWELVE BIGGEST MISTAKES SALESPEOPLE MAKE IN PRESENTATIONS
Patricia Fripp

SALESPEOPLE ARE LIKE HOLLYWOOD actors. Whenever they open their mouths, they are putting themselves and their companies on the line, taking a risk in the hope of a favorable outcome. Just like actors, even the best, most experienced salesperson can use some coaching and polishing now and then.

Here are the twelve most common mistakes that I see my sales clients make.

1. Unclear Thinking

If you can't describe the objective of your interaction in one sentence, you may be guilty of fuzzy focus, trying to say too much at once. You'll confuse your listener, and that doesn't make the sale.

Decide exactly what you want and need to accomplish in this contact. What would be a positive outcome? For example, imagine that a busy executive says, "You have exactly ten minutes of my time to tell me what you want me to know about your company. In one sentence, tell me how I should describe your benefits when I talk to my managers tomorrow." At any stage of the sales process, you should know in advance why you are interacting, what benefits you are offering your prospect or client, and what you'd like the next step to be.

2. No Clear Structure

Make it easy for your prospect to follow what you are saying, whether in a casual conversation or a formal presentation of information and ideas. They'll remember it better—and you will, too. Otherwise, you may forget to make a key point. If you waffle or ramble, you lose your listeners. Even for an informal presentation, mentally outline your objectives. What key "Points of Wisdom" do you want the prospect to remember? How will you illustrate each point? What colorful examples will your prospects be able to repeat three days later? What phrases or slogans do you want to guarantee they will repeat afterwards?

3. Talking Too Much

Salespeople often talk too much about themselves and their service or product. They make a speech rather than having an exchange or interaction, otherwise known as conversation. The key to connecting with a client is conversation; the secret of client conversation is to ask questions; the quality of client information received depends on the quality of the questions—and waiting for, and listening to, the answers.

In fact, a successful encounter early in the sales process should probably be mostly open-ended questions, the kind that require essay answers rather than just "yes" and "no." And don't rush on with preprogrammed questions that pay no attention to the answer you've just received. Learn to listen, even pausing to wait for further comments. *Silence draws people out.*

4. No Memorable Stories

People rarely remember your exact words. Instead, they remember the mental images your words inspire. Support your key points with vivid, relevant stories. Help them "make the movie" in their minds by using memorable characters, exciting situations, intriguing dialogue, suspense, and humor.

5. No Third-Person Endorsements

There's a limit to how many bold claims you can make about your company and product results, but there is no limit to the words of praise you can put in the mouths of your delighted clients. Use case histories of your clients' success stories about the benefits they received from your service or product.

When you are using their actual dialogue, you can say much more glowing things about yourself and your company than you could if the words were your own. Your endorsement stories should use the same ingredients as a good Hollywood movie: create memorable characters, use vivid dialogue, and provide a dramatic lesson learned. Choose characters that your prospects can connect with. It helps if the star of your story holds a similar position to your prospect.

You can't say, "Do business with me, and you'll be promoted," but you can give a specific example of someone who phoned, e-mailed, or wrote you that this happened to him or her. "Just last week," you might say, "I heard from Mary Smith. She's the payroll manager at Amalgamated Systems. She said that changing their payroll system to our company not only made them more efficient, but they cut their costs 10 percent. She told me, 'You made me look good in the eyes of management. Thanks to you, I received a promotion!'"

6. No Emotional Connection

The most powerful communication combines both intellectual and emotional connections. Intellectual means appealing to educated self-interest with data and reasoned arguments. Emotion comes from engaging the listeners' imaginations, involving them in your illustrative stories by frequent use of the word "you," and from answering their unspoken question, "What's in this for me?"

Obviously, a customer is going to justify doing business with you for specific analytical reasons. What gives you the edge—what I like to call the "unfair advantage"—is creating an emotional connection, too. Build this emotional connection by using stories with characters they can relate to and by providing a high I/you ratio, using the word "you" as often as possible and talking from the prospect's point of view.

My recommendation is that you make telephone appointments with your happiest clients. Tell them you would like to use their stories about working with you as an endorsement, and ask permission to record your conversation. Then just let them talk. The more they say, encouraged now and then by a question from you, the better their stories and quotes will be. Finally, select the best quotes from what they've said.

7. Wrong Level of Abstraction

Are you providing the big picture and generalities when your listeners are hungry for details, facts, and specific how-to's? Or are you drowning them in data when they need to position themselves with an overview and find out why they should care? Get on the same wavelength with your prospects. For first contacts with executives, describe what your company can do for them in broad generalities. With middle managers, discuss exactly how you can work together, a medium level of abstraction. If you are dealing with IT professionals, use the lowest level of abstraction, lots of facts and figures. Don't discuss aspects or details of what you're offering that your audience has no interest in.

8. No Pauses

Few sales presentations have enough pauses. Good music and good sales communication both contain changes of pace, pauses, and full rests. This is when listeners think about important points you've just made. If you rush on at full speed to crowd in as much information as possible, chances are you've left your prospects back at the station. Give them enough time to ask a question or even time to think over what has been said. Pauses allow pondering and understanding.

9. Irritating Non-Words

Hmm—ah—er—you know what I mean. One presenter I heard began each new thought with "Now!" as he scanned his notes to figure out what came next. This might be OK occasionally, but not every thirty seconds. Practice in front of your sales manager or colleagues, giving them permission to call out whenever you *hem* or *ah*. Or video or audiotape yourself, and note any digressions.

10. Stepping on the Punch Word

The most important word in a sentence is the punch word. Usually, this is the final word: "Take my wife—PLEASE." But if you drop your voice or add, "Right?" or "See?" or "You know?" or "OK?," you've killed the impact of your message.

Another popular punch-line killer is the word "today." Avoid saying, "Let's look at the recommendations we have for you *today*." Obviously, you're talking "today." The punch word in this sentence should be "recommendations." Comedian Jerry Seinfeld says, "I'll spend an hour reducing an eight-word sentence to five words because the joke will be funnier."

I train sales teams to do the same thing with their key phrases because their presentations will be more powerful. We go through their sentences, looking for the "$10 words." Not every word or phrase is, or should be, of equal importance. Emphasize the action words and phrases or those that make an emotional connection. "And" "it" "in" are no-dollar words. One sales team came up with what they called "$100 phrases," calling out, "Wow, that's SO good!" whenever someone used an especially potent phrase. Often it was a succinct term for a hard-to-describe benefit. Such a phrase can be priceless.

For example, a company offering a complex process might explain, "We're like a security guard who keeps the bad guys out and lets the good guys in." To find $100 phrases for your company, I suggest this process: Imagine you're trying to explain what you do to your eighty-two-year-old great aunt. How you describe it should be part of your conversational sales presentation. This is an especially good technique to use for executive overviews. If your $100 phrase is "visual enough," your prospects and clients will repeat it later.

11. Not Having Strong Openings and Closings

Engage your audience immediately with a powerful, relevant opening that includes them. For example, "You have an awesome responsibility." Then fill in what it is: increasing sales, reducing errors, cutting overhead—whatever your product can help your prospect do.

Another excellent strategy is to do some research. Then you can say, "Congratulations on your company's recent success" and describe it. Or "I love your new commercials." Most salespeople start by talking about their company. *Talk about your prospect instead.* Whenever I give a speech for a company, I check out their website, corporate reports, or press releases to find something their chairman of the board or CEO has said that I can quote.

You can do this, too, making it almost sound as if their CEO is recommending your company. For example, "Our core values are . . ." and match them to your own. Or "We subscribe to *Best Practices*, and all our preferred vendors do as well." That's you!

To close, pick the one sentence that you absolutely want embedded in their minds, even if you don't get the appointment or the sale. Leave them with a strong, positive message. They might say, "We're happy with our present vendor." You reply, "I appreciate your LOYALTY [a $10 word]. If you ever want a SECOND vendor [$10 word] or for any reason they DISSATISFY [$10 word] you, you need to do business with a company that will be around LONG-TERM [$10 word]. Please remember, we've been PROFIT-ABLE [$10 word] for the last 167 quarters [$10 word]." In the search for $100 phrases, don't just add up $10 words. A $100 phrase stands alone.

12. Misusing Technology

Too many salespeople rely too much on their PowerPoint and flip charts and not enough on making an emotional connection. Charles H. Green, co-author of *The Trusted Advisor*, tells about four advertising agencies who were given an opportunity to bid for a large account. Each group had two hours. The last team walked in and said, "We're ready to do exactly what the other three competing agencies have done. We can give you the Dance of a Thousand Slides, but you have a choice. You can pretend you already hired us, and for the next two hours we can start brainstorming on your account. If you hire us, you've received two free hours of consultation, and if you don't, you've still had two hours free."

They proved they could think on their feet and be flexible. This won them a very profitable account. They showed they could use the latest technology, but, more important, that they didn't need it. "Whenever you're being considered for a job," says Charlie, "act as if you already have it. Most people want to think that the quality of their work speaks for itself. It doesn't. Beat your competition by getting to work for your prospect immediately. Demonstrate how it will feel to be working together."

All four agencies could have done a fine job. The one that landed the account had enough confidence in its presentation skills to use technology or not. The client was exhilarated by their work session, impressed by the agency's flexibility, and confident this agency would and could do a great job.

Many sales teams couldn't communicate with a prospect for two hours without the help of a suitcase full of charts, PowerPoint slides, and electronic equipment.

When you learn to avoid these twelve common presentation traps, you're on your way to being a "star" of the sales world, ready to accept an award for your dazzling performance.

Patricia Fripp (www.fripp.com) is a San Francisco–based executive speech coach, sales trainer, and award-winning keynote speaker.

•   •   •

HOW TO CUSTOMIZE GENERIC POWERPOINT SLIDES FOR SALES PROSPECTS
Dave Paradi

A PROSPECT FROM A COMPANY that is an ideal customer for your product or service has a specific problem he is losing sleep over. He sees one of your generic ads in an industry trade publication and it interests him enough to visit your website. At the website, he reads more detailed information, and it looks promising, so he contacts a sales rep.

The sales rep meets with the prospect to find out specifics on the problem. The rep leaves behind a generic brochure. The prospect heard enough promising information from the rep that he decides to invite the rep to present to a larger audience of key decision-makers.

What kind of content is your marketing department going to provide the rep for this vital presentation? Too often, the answer is a generic set of slides. And that's going to be a problem—for the rep and for the decision-makers at the prospect company.

The sales rep knows she needs a customized presentation to meet the specific needs of the situation. So she'll do one of two things. Either she'll use the generic presentation and fumble through it as she skips the parts she doesn't need. Or she'll create her own set of slides and likely present poorly designed versions that don't match the important branding the marketing department has worked hard to create.

Neither approach results in a successful presentation and neither gives the sales rep a good chance of securing the order.

What the rep really needs is a customized presentation that is consistent with the corporate branding. It should be primarily visual so that she can talk about the specific needs of the prospect and relate how her products and services have solved problems similar to the ones the prospect is facing. It looks professional and gives the impression that if prospects accept your proposal, they are going with a firm that stands behind what it says.

Yeah, right. *Who has the manpower or time in their marketing department to create a custom set of slides for every sales presentation?* No one does. So what are you to do?

The solution is to create a partnership whereby marketing provides sales with the tools and training to create consistently customized visual (CCV) presentations every time. The key is to tap the strengths of each party when approaching the prospect. Marketing brings the consistent branding skills and key messages, and sales reps bring the knowledge of the prospect's specific needs.

Here are the steps you can follow to develop CCV presentations in your firm.

Step 1: Create a Library of Standard Slides

The marketing department, in consultation with the sales staff, creates a library of slides that capture the key messages that the sales professionals use most often. This library consists of visual slides—employing carefully chosen photos and graphics instead of overloaded text slides—and is consistent with the branding of the company.

The library is not intended to cover every slide a sales rep would ever want to use, but will usually end up providing 70 to 80 percent of the slides for each sales presentation. This step provides each presentation with consistent branding and key messages using visuals.

Step 2: Train the Sales Staff on How to Use the Slide Library

Once the library of slides is created, the sales staff needs to know how and why to use it. The benefit of the library is that, by picking and choosing from the already created slides, salespeople will be able to rapidly assemble about three-quarters of their presentations.

Since most sales reps and support staff don't know how to use a slide library, they will need to be given simple instructions on how to select slides from the list and generate a new presentation. There is a range of tools to help facilitate this task, ranging from using a simple file of slides on the company intranet to specific web-based packages that manage content enterprise-wide. It is usually easiest to start with a simple approach first.

Step 3: Educate the Sales Staff on How to Create Visual Slides

Using the library will still leave the sales reps with about one-quarter of their own slides to create. They now need to be trained on how to create customized slides that have the same look and graphic approach as the library slides.

This doesn't require training on graphics design packages. Rather, it means showing them how to use the already designed "look" to the slides and helping them see how a visual can persuade better than a slide full of bulleted text.

Some firms even go as far as creating template slides for certain sales concepts that enable their staffs to pick a pre-designed slide and fill in the required text or graphic. This step adds the customized visuals that make the presentation laser-focused for each situation.

Step 4: Evaluate and Update the Library Every Four Months

Once the training is over and the library is in use, regular evaluation is needed. Are the sales reps able to use the library easily? Are there slides that they would like to see added to the library? Is additional training needed on the "how-to" aspect of creating slides and presentations?

This feedback should be used to update the library every four months. If additional training is needed, make it as specific as possible by canvassing the sales reps and addressing the topics they need to learn in as short a time as possible. You may also want to provide short "how-to" videos on the corporate intranet as reminders of the key techniques.

Dave Paradi runs the Think Outside the Slide website (www.thinkoutsidetheslide .com), is a consultant on high-stakes presentations, the author of seven books, and a PowerPoint Most Valuable Professional (MVP).

• • •

SIX WAYS TO BOOST RESULTS FROM TEAM SALES PRESENTATIONS
Steve Mandel

SOME OF THE HIGHEST STAKES sales opportunities require a team selling approach.

In the selling process, a sales team often must deliver one or many sales presentations—as a team—to small or large groups of customer decision-makers and influencers. But far too often, sales teams make the extraordinarily costly mistake of not investing enough time and thought in advance to prepare as a team to ensure a winning outcome for their presentations.

As a result, many team presentations communicate a disjointed, unimpressive message about the team and its value to the customer. In competitive situations, team presentation deficiencies become truly dire.

To gain the greatest chance of success, team presentations require a great deal of planning and practice—much more so than the single-presenter variety.

To help assure your team's success, I have outlined six of the pivotal areas that require the team's intense attention long before it ever ventures into the presentation room.

1. Enhance and Focus the Team's Knowledge

Whatever account strategy and call planning tools you have chosen to use, utilize them thoroughly to prepare for team presentations. At the very least, be sure each team member has

- A thorough understanding of the customer's organizational and individual needs

- Information about the wants and needs, receptivity, roles, responsibilities, and varying technical competency levels of the individual customer representatives to whom the presentation will be made

- Clear, relevant presentation objectives for everyone on the team

- Coordinated, cohesive, and compelling presentation content

- A clear understanding of the role that each sales team member will play in the presentation room

Each team member needs to be thoroughly prepared to confidently engage with the audience, support the team, and move the customer to the desired action.

2. Coordinate Around a Theme

A strong team presentation requires an overriding theme to give it customer-centric focus and continuity. The presentation should not be a disjointed series of talks by several presenters, each focusing—without much mutual connection—solely on one individual's area of expertise.

Carefully build each individual's section of the team presentation and then use it to link those individual presentations together. You want to ensure that all team members' individual presentations are soundly constructed and are tied together to flow cohesively and convincingly as a complete story for the listeners.

3. Practice to Ensure Excellence

A team sales presentation made without rehearsal sessions is like a world-class athletic team or concert orchestra trying to perform without practicing. The pros know the value of practice and rehearsal. They make it a major part of their professional lives.

Practice and rehearsal are no less essential in high-stakes selling situations—perhaps even more so.

Practice out loud, on your feet, with your team to prepare for each team presentation. Practice transitions or "handoffs" between individual presenters and interactions with supporting media. Arrange for in-the-moment coaching by a skillful manager or a professional presentation coach during your practices. Your team's success deserves nothing less.

4. Pick Your Team Leader with Care

The assignment of a presentation team leader is an important step. The presentation team leader is often, but not always, the account manager or account executive. Make the leader selection explicit.

The team leader's role includes the responsibility for gathering and sharing insightful information about the customer's business, organization, and people. The leader also gives guidance to the sales team about the presentation's objectives, the strategic and tactical situation, personalities, needs, styles, competitive situation, and critical successful factors.

The team leader may also help the individual presenters coordinate their sections to emphasize audience needs and arrange for the required amount of presentation practice and coaching.

The team leader is often the central focus for the customer and should be the person to whom customer representatives have already granted some trust and credibility—and with whom they have shared most fully their needs for business solutions.

As such, the team leader is also the person the client or prospect is likely to contact with additional requests, concerns, questions, or objections after the sales presentation.

It typically is the team leader's responsibility to open the overall presentation, deliver some portion of the content, field questions along with others, as appropriate, and close the presentation with summaries and next steps.

The team leader should be a leader in the truest sense. He or she needs to understand the strategic value and tactical essentials of successful team presentations.

5. Understand the Environment

If possible, practice in or become familiar with the environment in which you will be presenting. When that is not possible, arrive early and gain as much of a sense of the locale and layout as you can before you need to start.

At the very least, if the assignments are known beforehand, ask your customer contact to describe the room and seating arrangements planned for your team's presentation.

Be sure to ask well beforehand for any particular seating arrangements that you would prefer and for any presentation equipment you will need, for example, projector screens, flip charts, whiteboards, etc. (Carry your own team back-up items when possible. It's hard to use a customer's flip chart, for example, when no one has remembered to provide markers for you.)

Position the presentation team members strategically in the room. If given flexibility, manage your environment to work to your team's advantage.

Each environment and situation is different, so adjust accordingly.

As a general guideline, place yourselves so that (1) no team member will distract customer attention from the team member who is presenting at any point in time and (2) you're in a place where each team member who may need to interact with the audience can do so naturally, as appropriate, when not presenting.

Whether the team sits together or is seated among the customers attending the presentation is a judgment call.

6. Remember: Your Team Is Never Offstage

Don't consider yourself offstage at any time during the team's presentation.

Your customers are not only evaluating your content during a team sales presentation, but they are also watching and listening to see how your team members treat each other. Decision-makers often consider your team interactions to be valuable previews of how your organization is likely to treat them if they elect to do business with you.

Consequently, whenever you make a change from presenter to presenter, the way that each team member makes those transitions will become a focal point for your audience. Make sure you introduce the next presenter in a positive, respectful, and friendly way.

Be enthusiastic. Smile and make eye contact with the next presenter on your team. She or he should acknowledge the introduction by saying at least "Thank you" or "Thanks, Jim. I'd like to pick up where Jim just left off by discussing the idea of. . . ."

Act as though you are proud to be introducing or following your colleague. Get the audience excited about what's to come. Be aware: Your audience will also be observing what you personally are doing when you are not presenting.

Make sure you are not appearing disinterested in the customer or disconnected from the presentation by gazing out the window or at your shoes. Please, please never check your cell phone or iPad while in a sales presentation room, even if you think no one will catch you, because someone inevitably will (and you probably won't know it either).

Pay close attention to your colleagues when they are presenting, even if you have heard it a thousand times before. (Avoid artificially nodding and smiling at everything that's said though. Be sincerely engaged.)

Last, remember that most people—whenever they can justify it—buy from people they like (even if they don't know those people very well).

Thoroughly plan and practice as a team so you can be relaxed and engaged with the customer before, during, and after the team's presentation. Make your sales team the people with whom others want to do business.

Steve Mandel is founder and president of Mandel Communications (www.mandel .com), a presentation skills coaching company in Capitola, California.

• • •

GETTING PROPOSAL GRAPHICS RIGHT THE FIRST TIME
Mike Parkinson

DO THESE COMPLAINTS sound familiar?

- "Our sales proposal graphics need to be better."
- "I have to explain things over and over again."
- "Our graphics take too long to develop and cost too much."
- "My presentation design team isn't on the same page."

You're not alone. These are issues that my company frequently encounters when starting a new sales proposal. To overcome these challenges, I created six mitigating strategies. These strategies can save you time and money, reduce hassles, and increase your chances of winning the pitch.

When you apply any of the six strategies to your proposal, you should see a decrease in team stress and an increase in production speed. The design process will be more enjoyable and your team will deliver more communicative, successful graphics faster than before.

1. Make the Designers Part of Your Team

Everyone on the team should share the same vision, mission, and goals. For that reason, involve the graphic designers as early as possible. Make them a part of your sales proposal team. No piece of the proposal should be regarded as insignificant.

Like authors, designers communicate vital information. The less they know about the proposal, the less likely they are to communicate the right message and the more likely that there will be miscommunication and lengthy reiterations of the same graphic. To ignore this fact is to give your competitor the advantage and drive both your production and authoring costs higher.

The designers (as well as the rest of the team) must know the roles they play, what is expected of them, and the "big picture." What are the audience's goals and challenges? What are the customer's hot buttons? What terms or imagery does the customer prefer or dislike?

Involve the designers early and make them part of your team to increase the value of their contributions. The benefits are often incalculable.

2. Storyboard

Storyboard your project. Agree to the outline, stories, messages, solutions, and themes that will be shared in the proposal before writing and developing graphics. Have the designer create graphics (sketches or mockups are sufficient) that address the solutions proposed for each of the proposal sections or slides.

This design-first technique will allow all authors to quickly and easily write to the same depiction of the solution. For example, which would you rather write a presentation to, Graphic A or B in Figure 8.1?

Figure 8.1. Graphic vs. Text Presentation

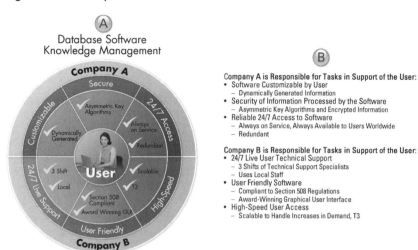

"If you cannot picture it, you cannot write about it," says Mike Conk, who has worked in the proposal industry for more than twenty years. Developing an overview graphic forces the presentation authors to analyze the information and organize it in a way that is logical, easy to follow, and easier to write to.

The more information revealed during storyboarding, the lower the risk of lengthy rewrites and wasted graphics. Finding a story and solution that everyone agrees to during storyboarding is a key to creating graphics right the first time.

3. Leverage Existing Graphics

The third strategy is leveraging existing graphics to create new, project-specific visuals. Typically, authors have an existing process, tool, and/or approach for handling each topic discussed in the proposal. Aspects will need to be tailored for the current audience, but starting with something that has worked in the past is a smart move.

Most PowerPoint users struggle with thinking graphically. Attempting to develop slides with no more than a blank screen is unnecessarily challenging and time-consuming.

Instead, start with an existing image of a solution that worked in the past. This step will save hours and reduce stress, and the solution will be more thoughtful (benefiting from past insights, other perspectives, and audience feedback).

Picasso once said, "Good artists copy, but great artists steal." In other words, be smart and use what others before you have learned, while still honoring copyright law.

4. Evolve the Concept Before Rendering the Final Graphic

Proposals often require long days with limited resources, driven by tight deadlines. If there is no time or money to evolve the graphic, sketch or mock up the concept first. Present it to the author for approval. When possible, have the concept reviewed by people who are similar to your target audience. If everyone agrees that the concept works, the graphic can be rendered. If not, tweak the sketch or mockup until everyone agrees.

The graphic, like the one in Figure 8.2, is now ready to be rendered on the computer.

Figure 8.2.   Graphic Prior to Computer Conversion

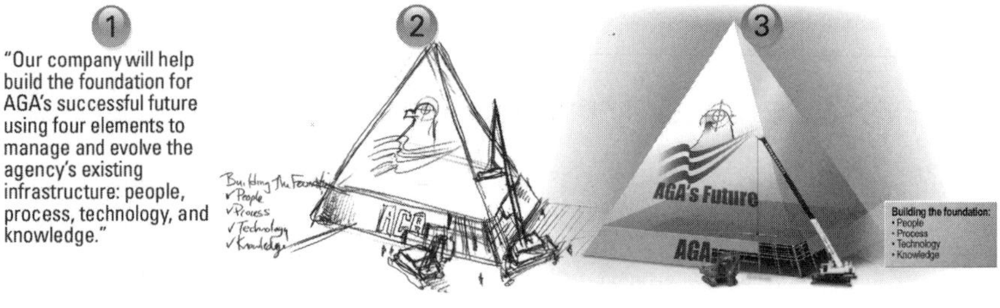

5. Use a Template

Using a template such as the one in Figure 8.3 reduces the need for last-minute formatting passes. It works every time. Agree to and use

a template that defines all variables of the graphics at the beginning
of the project:

- Color (primary, secondary, tertiary)
- Fonts (style for titles, subtitles, graphics, and content)
- Graphic style (that is, vector, raster, silhouettes, and effects)
- Lines
- Capitalization (bullets, titles, and content)
- Arrows
- Log numbers
- Proposal requirements (e.g., corporate style guidelines)

Figure 8.3.   Template for Slide Design

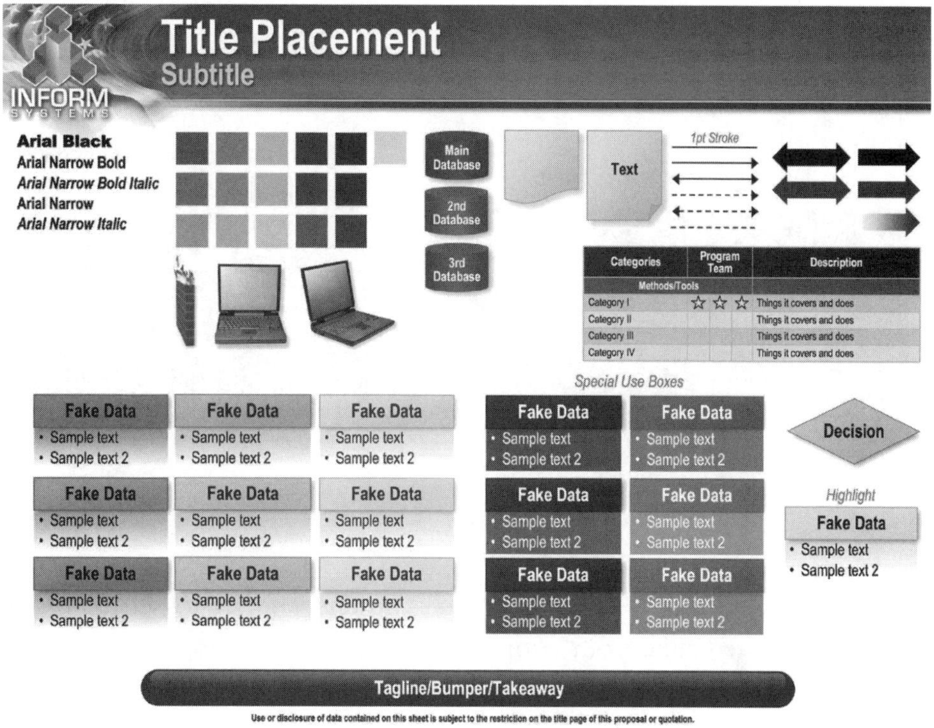

Make sure the proposal lead and/or presentation proposal
manager reviews the template before a designer renders graphics.

Ensure all designers strictly adhere to the approved template to keep graphics consistent and significantly limit the number of formatting revisions.

6. Make Graphics Customer-Focused

Last, the authors and designers must make the graphics customer-focused, like those in Figure 8.4. What is it about the presented information that is of importance to the audience?

Make it obvious. Studies have proven that graphics communicate faster and are remembered better than text alone. Use this to your advantage. For example, create a graphic that highlights your features, benefits, and discriminators.

Figure 8.4.   Graphic Using Customer's Needs

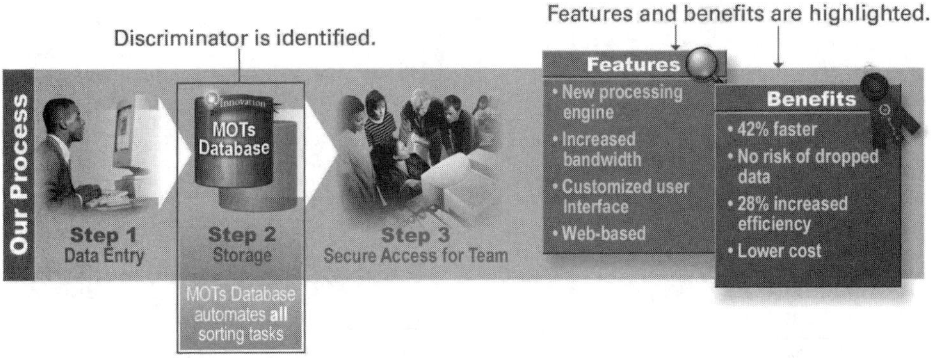

Concentrate on what your audience needs to see, read, and hear to make your proposal successful. Ignoring your audience in favor of your own agenda results in poor graphics and a losing proposal. The audience wants to know how the presented information benefits them. If that benefit is clear, the audience will stay attentive.

Follow these six strategies and you will find that getting graphics right the first time pays great dividends. You will save time and money, reduce stress, and win more sales proposals.

Mike Parkinson is the CEO of Billion Dollar Graphics (www.billiondollargraphics .com), an internationally recognized visual communication expert and a multi-published author in the presentations field.

• • •

BRINGING OUT THE ACTOR WITHIN
David Zielinski

ACTING. PRETENDING. Assuming another persona. Checking your identity at the door and slipping into someone else's skin. Conventional wisdom tells us this is the modus operandi of successful stage and TV actors. We're also led to believe it's the process used by many good speakers, communicators, and salespeople.

To effectively sell products or services during your presentations, you often have to become a larger version of yourself. Acting instructors and speech coaches say that "bringing out the actor within" does include plenty of acting secrets, but mainly it's about getting to know yourself better.

Actors—and presenters—never truly reach their potential, they say, until they find out what's special about their own styles and stop trying to parrot others' styles. "Most people think acting is pretending," says Jan D'Arcy, an executive speech coach and professional actor whose credits include popular American television shows such as "The X-Files" and "Twin Peaks."

"Acting and, to a large extent, speaking, are both about self-revelation," she says. "The successful performer always searches for the truth in herself, and then uses dramatic means to present the truth to the audience. So the more you're aware of your own identity, the more powerful you'll be as a presenter. When people ask what I do as a presentation skill coach, I don't say I package people. I unwrap them."

The essence of much modern acting, say acting instructors and speech coaches, is based on realism and authenticity. The moment anyone is identified as a phony, that person is usually dead in the water.

Repeat Messaging Requires Acting

All of us "act" repeatedly throughout our workdays, and that's doubly true for those speaking to an audience. Each time we repeat a communication effort or message, we become actors in a sense. The first time you deliver that message, you're a communicator, acting coaches say. The third or fourth time, you are essentially acting.

Good actors are believable only to the extent that they're in touch with their own authentic feelings. Conjuring up past experiences and emotions, rather than trying to manufacture them in a vacuum, is known in the acting profession as "The Method" or sense memory.

Sense memory can help speakers build a more engaging stage presence, D'Arcy says. "When you're walking up to speak to the audience, you want to find a sense memory, a visualization, of those times you felt especially good, when you were confident and in control," she says. It might be the time you received kudos for a job performance, gave a well-received impromptu speech at a wedding reception, or were recognized publicly and represented yourself well accepting the honor.

Speakers in the corporate arena often mistakenly believe they only have to communicate ideas and words, D'Arcy says. The truth is that presenters and salespeople, like actors, also have to communicate emotions and energy to capture an audience—or to win over sales prospects.

Developing an Authentic Presence

Although you might glean ideas from the speaking styles of Steve Jobs or Tony Robbins, the last thing you should do is try to remake yourself in another speaker's image. Audiences don't want presenters all to sound or look alike.

So how can you find your authentic stage presence without spending hours on a psychotherapist's couch? If you view yourself as naturally reticent or undemonstrative, how can you feel comfortable as a more animated and emotive presenter, especially when presenting to sales prospects?

D'Arcy suggests these tactics to help unleash the actor within:

1. Ramp up your rehearsal time. "Actors spend weeks in rehearsal before they even dare get up on stage—and they have the advantage of a director guiding them," she says. "I see speakers who think they can just get up and be brilliant after one run-through. But if you fail to use any skill often enough, it won't improve."

   Some presenters fear repeated rehearsal will make them look and sound robotic. Quite the contrary, says D'Arcy. While mindless drilling helps no one, well-planned rehearsal—focused as much on personal stories, slide transitions, and pacing as on reciting PowerPoint slide text—eases anxiety and greases the skids for improvisation or enlightening asides in a speech.

2. Take an acting class or become involved in community theater. "Community theater also teaches that you have to perform even when you have a cold, just left your crying children at home, or received a traffic ticket," D'Arcy says.

David Zielinski is the editor of PresentationXpert newsletter, www.presentation-xpert.com. This article was adapted from an article that first appeared in *Toastmaster* magazine.

• • •

WE ARE PROGRAMMED TO FORGET . . . AND HOW IT IMPACTS SALES DEMOS
Peter Cohan

WE ARE INDEED programmed to forget—and consider the impact this has on traditional software demonstrations.

Imagine you are driving home from work or on an errand . . . what do you remember about the cars and signs you see, the roadside debris, people, buildings, and the roads you pass? How much of that information is retained?

Very little is actually remembered about what you saw along your way. Our brains are continuously evaluating what we see and hear as we move through our day—and continuously discarding anything that is not considered important, threatening, or particularly interesting.

What don't we remember? Everything that is typical, expected, or normal.

What do we remember? Remarkable events, problems, danger and close calls, humor (things that made us laugh), anger (things that made us mad), and other emotional experiences (things that caused a strong emotional reaction).

What's Forgotten?

How does this impact our sales demos and what presentation audiences remember? In an hour-long traditional sales demo, we shouldn't expect our audiences to remember very much:

- They won't remember long sequences of features, functions, and options.

- They won't remember complex workflows, loops, and multiple "if" cases.
- They won't remember the confusing interdependencies of configuration choices, multiple roles, and intertwined pathways.

What's Remembered?

What will audiences recall from traditional demos? The beginning, the end, and the ugly:

- They will remember the first and last few things that are shown.
- They will remember the bugs, crashes, ignored or poorly handled questions, the amusing distractions from other audience members, and particularly stunning fumbling for features.
- And they will remember an overall impression of the demo as being boring, confusing, or complicated.

They may also remember the absence of capabilities they were looking for—in many cases, even if these capabilities were, in fact, presented!

What Can We Do to Improve Success Rates?

Here are three simple tactics to help your customers retain the key ideas you want them to remember:

1. Shall we all say it together? "Do the last thing first!" When presented with a long list of ideas, people remember the first few items very well and the last few items moderately well, and the material in between generally is lost. This is the "attention-retention" principle.

Take advantage of this and start your demos with the most compelling, most interesting deliverables for each audience. If the audience remembers nothing else, they will remember the most important part of your demo—the payoff, the visual evidence of the solution to their problem.

2. People absorb and retain information best when it is presented in discrete "chunks," as opposed to a long linear flow. Organize and present your demos accordingly—in consumable components—and use a roadmap to help manage the delivery of your component chunks.

3. Adults learn by repetition—so when you complete a demo segment, summarize. Repeat, verbally, what you just showed them. If you are face-to-face, you should see your audience nodding their heads, which means they have heard you, they understand, and they have a higher likelihood of remembering.

How can you tell whether your audience will remember the key points? You'll see them making notes—writing things down.

We combat our "programming-to-forget" by making notes of the major ideas, issues, and questions we want to remember. For software demos, if you are doing well, you'll see your audience making notes about key capabilities and writing comments about what they find particularly interesting.

I Really Remember . . .

What else can we do to help audiences remember our demos? Anything that is perceived as remarkable is memorable. For example:

- *Provide a unique presentation of a solution to a problem.* "Wow! They showed us the key reports that we need to produce right up-front at the beginning of their demo. And they showed generating those reports in three mouse clicks, as opposed to what is taking us a week to do today. . . !"
- *Engage the audience.* "That was so cool. They had John drive a portion of their demo, and John still types in all caps. . . !"
- *Develop concepts or materials ad hoc.* "It was great when they built a new form for us, first on a whiteboard and then right in their software!"

- *Make it a two-way conversation.* "We were really engaged—asking questions and even coming up with new ideas for our process."
- *Finish the demo early.* "Wow! They finished early and I had time to get some real work done!"
- *Be humorous, but effective.* "It was funny when the sales guy said, 'The bad news is I have a sixty-slide corporate overview presentation to show—the good news is that I'm not going to inflict it on you.'"
- *Use props.* "Do you remember when their technical guy came into the room with this huge stack of documents and folders spilling all over the place? Looked like our day-to-day lives to me!"
- *Run their examples.* "That was really nice. We rarely take something of value away from a sales demo."

Humans are, by nature, programmed to forget. Causatively forgetting the unimportant, the uninteresting, and the unremarkable is how our brains are able to handle the enormous volume of information we encounter every day.

Make your demos memorable by doing the last thing first, organizing your delivery in consumable components, and by summarizing—as basics. Make your demos truly unforgettable by doing the unexpected, the noteworthy, and the remarkable.

Peter Cohan is principal of The Second Derivative (www.secondderivative.com), a company that specializes in helping clients improve their sales demonstration effectiveness skills.

The Power of Story

HONING YOUR STORYTELLING SKILLS

The research is in, and if making a lasting impact on your audience is the goal, you'd do well to consider it: audiences remember a brief, well-told story much longer than bullet points on a slide or data in a bar graph. While the latter are integral to good presentations, stories and narrative connected to your key messages make a bigger emotional impact, receive closer attention, and are remembered longer by audiences.

Because they are visual and stimulate the viewer's imagination, stories cause the non-linear right brain to engage—connecting the emotional to the intellectual—and the best of these tales usually come from your own personal experiences.

Like any other skill, telling stories requires study and repeated practice to achieve mastery. But once learned, storytelling becomes a potent arrow in your presentations quiver.

• • •

THE FIRST FIVE SLIDES: UNLOCKING THE STORY BURIED IN YOUR PRESENTATION
Cliff Atkinson

I F YOU USE BULLET POINTS in your PowerPoint presentations, it's probably because writing bullets helps you to build slides quickly and reminds you to cover all the points you want to make. Although bullet points may help you to do many things, one thing they cannot do is help you to tell a story.

Some of the world's largest organizations today have adopted the *word story* as their new mantra for corporate communications. Marketing messages should tell a story, corporate strategy should tell a story, mission statements should tell a story, and even websites should tell a story.

Why the sudden interest in story? For one clue, look no further than the approach you may be applying to your own PowerPoint slides, which lock out the possibility of telling a story in the first place.

The Origin of Bullet Points

The origin of bullet points in presentations is actually clearly visible on most PowerPoint slides—a type of outlining approach that everyone uses, yet no one questions. This approach always begins by placing a category heading at the top of a slide, such as Our History, Challenges, Outlook, and Lessons Learned.

It is remarkable that you see exactly the same headings in every presentation, across organizations, professions, and even cultures. These headings do nothing more than establish a category of information, which you then explain with a bulleted list below it. Although this approach can help you create slides quickly, it also guarantees that you never do anything more than present a series of lists to an audience.

When the primary way that we communicate is by presenting lists to one another, it is no wonder that the phenomenon of story is gaining momentum, because a story is the opposite of a list. Where a list is dry, fragmented, and soulless; a story is juicy, coherent, and full of life. Presented with the choice, *any audience will choose life.*

So that leaves us with the essential problem: If we can agree that the era of the story is dawning, and that bullet points are standing in our way, how do we unlock the power of a story in our PowerPoint presentations?

This is becoming an issue of strategic concern to major players of large organizations in which PowerPoint has replaced the written word as the predominant way of communicating information. To find the answer, we only have to look forward as far as the past.

What Kind of a Story?

The concept of a story may be a new idea to the boardroom, but storytelling is at least as old as the person who defined it as an art 2,400 years ago—Aristotle. If you think Aristotle's ideas on story are no longer relevant, look no further than a movie screen. Hollywood screenwriters still credit Aristotle with writing the definitive elements of story: action, a plot, central characters, and visual effects.

But even Aristotle knew that not all stories are created equal, so the natural question arises: Exactly what kind of story is appropriate for a presentation? For example, a story can take the shape of a Hollywood blockbuster meant to entertain, or a story can be a colorful anecdote about something that happened on vacation. Although both are stories, neither is complete enough to fulfill the complex needs of presenters and audiences today, who need much more than entertainment or personal anecdotes in order to make fully informed decisions.

Instead, today we need a specific type of story that blends together a classical story structure along with classical ideas about persuasion. Again, Aristotle offers a great deal to the discussion because he wrote the book on persuasion in addition to the book on storytelling.

In order to bring Aristotle's classical ideas up-to-date in a media-savvy world, you need to blend one part storytelling, one part persuasion, and one part Hollywood screenwriting to create a powerful approach for your PowerPoint presentations.

Unlocking the Secret Code of Persuasive Stories

A persuasive story uses the structure of a story, but spins the story in a particular way that ensures it aims at achieving clear results. You can apply this fundamental structure to any type of presentation, and combining it with a visual medium such as PowerPoint helps you tap into additional levels of communicative power that Hollywood shows us every day.

For example, let's see how a persuasive story looks in the form of the first five slides in a PowerPoint presentation to a board of directors, where the presenter is seeking approval for a new product.

Instead of using a category heading, the top of each slide features a simple statement that addresses each category of information that the board needs to know about the story, as described here.

Slide 1: Establish the Setting

The headline of Slide 1 reads: *Our sector of business is undergoing major change.* The subject of this headline establishes the common setting for the presentation and relates the "where" and "when" for everyone in the audience.

Slide 2: Designate the Audience as the Main Character

The headline of Slide 2 reads: *Every board faces tough decisions about what to do next.* The subject of this headline establishes the members of the board as the main characters of this story, establishing the "who" of the story.

Slide 3: Describe a Conflict Involving the Audience

The headline of Slide 3 reads: *Six new products have eroded our market share.* The subject of this headline describes a conflict the board faces that has created an imbalance, in the form of the erosion of market share. This explains "why" the audience is there—to solve the problem.

Slide 4: Explain the Audience's Desired State

The headline of Slide 4 reads: *We can regain profitability by launching a new product.* The board doesn't want to stay in a state of imbalance, so the subject of this headline describes the board's desired state, describing "what" the audience wants to see happen.

Slide 5: Recommend a Solution

The headline of Slide 5 reads: *Approve the plan to build Product X and we'll reach our goals.* This final headline recommends a solution, describing "how" the audience will go from their current state of imbalance to their desired state of balance.

Reading these five headlines in succession reveals an interesting and engaging story that will be sure to capture the board's attention. When you add an illustration to each of these headlines, you open up the power of projected images, including full-screen photographs, clip art, or even simple animated words.

The Rest of the Story

The five slides in this example form the backbone of Act I of a persuasive story structure. Act II then spins off of the pivotal fifth slide, explaining the various reasons why the audience should accept the solution. Act III frames the resolution, setting the stage for the audience to decide whether to accept the recommended solution.

With the solid structure of your first five slides in place, your presentations will move well beyond the stale world of bullet points and into the lively world of a persuasive story.

Cliff Atkinson is a writer, keynote speaker, and presentations consultant to CEOs who wrote the bestselling book *Beyond Bullet Points* (www.beyondbulletpoints .com). He used his method to create the presentations that helped persuade a jury to award a $253 million verdict to the plaintiff in the nation's first Vioxx trial.

• • •

WHY SOME STORIES WORK AND OTHERS FALL FLAT
Doug Stevenson

AS THE WAITERS CLEARED the dessert plates from the banquet tables, Joanne, the vice president of sales, stepped to the podium and began the annual meeting. The CEO, Jeff Carlson, could feel the heat building under his collar. He wiped his sweaty palms on the linen napkin and took another sip of water to wet his cottonmouth lips.

Joanne welcomed everyone with charm and candor. She got a few laughs with a short story about the Region 3 delivery truck that was impounded for parking illegally. Then came the moment when she introduced Jeff.

As he moved toward the podium, Jeff felt time stand still. The room was dark except for the spotlight, which felt to Jeff like a heat lamp beaming on his face. He glanced down at his notes, made a funny comment about the driver of the truck, and then, with hands shaking almost uncontrollably, launched into his speech.

Afterward, as his mental acuity returned to normal, he asked his wife how he did. He really didn't know. It was as if he wasn't there during the speech, at least not as the confident and secure CEO that he knew himself to be.

Picking Up Your Power

Jeff knew instinctively that something was missing when he spoke in front of a group. After observing the confidence and poise of the guest speaker who followed him, he finally put a name to it: *his power.* In every other aspect of his life, he was a confident and powerful man. But when he stepped in front of a room full of people to speak, he lost connection to that power.

Does that happen to you? Do you feel the same level of confidence and power while giving a speech as you do while running your company or department? If not, it's time to learn an important skill that will make sure you retain your power on the platform: *strategic storytelling.*

Storytelling is a powerful leadership tool. It puts you in touch with your authentic power so you can motivate and inspire your audience. Professional speakers have learned how to turn storytelling into an art form. They know they can both connect with their audience and deliver vital messages using the power of storytelling.

Stories are the perfect form of communication working on many levels. Because they are inherently visual and stimulate the imagination, stories cause the non-linear right brain to engage; because the sequence of the story is linear, they cause the left linear brain to engage. Stories are emotional as well as educational, thus connecting the head and the heart. They are well received by auditory, visual, and kinesthetic learners because well-crafted stories can incorporate all modes of learning. In short, stories are the window through which audience members see their own truth.

Why then, do some stories work and others don't? The answer lies in the art of storytelling. Almost any story has the potential to be a great story. The secret is in choosing and crafting a story for its strategic use.

Here are a few criteria to apply to using stories in your business presentations.

Share Personal Stories

Audience members want to know who you are and what you believe. Stories from your life humanize you and make you more approachable. They reveal the person beneath the title. Research affirms that people follow leaders they trust and believe in. By sharing personal stories that teach lessons from your life, you reveal the source of your wisdom as a leader.

Before listeners buy into what you have to say, they have to buy *you*. You are the message. Given that, the next question becomes: What's your story?

Make a Point

When told in front of business audiences, stories have to make a point, so strive to match the point you want to make to the story you tell before you begin.

But be careful. *Never attach a point to a story that doesn't fit naturally.* The point should flow effortlessly out of the story. When you know the point you want to teach, ask yourself: "Where did I learn that lesson?"

Search for stories from your own life and fan out from there. Start crafting your story with your key point in mind. Here's an example. In one of my keynote talks, I teach the value of focusing on solutions instead of problems by telling a story about running late for a speech in Kansas City. My plane had been delayed and, to make matters worse, when I finally arrived at the airport, I missed the only shuttle that would have taken me to my appointment on time.

So I spotted a limo at the curbside and, out of desperation, asked the driver if he could give me a ride. His other passenger had just cancelled so he said yes.

By focusing on the solution, I saw the limo, took action, and got to my appointment on time. Had I focused on the problem, I would have waited for the next shuttle and been late. I wouldn't have seen the opportunity for an innovative solution.

This key point flows out of my limo story and, at the end, I suggest that when things don't work out the way they're supposed to, then "Look for the limo."

The Magic Is in the Details

To stimulate your listeners' imaginations, be sure to craft your stories with rich detail. Remember and relate every nuance, every character, and every emotion. Was someone driving a car or an old beat-up Chevy with spongy shock absorbers that made it shimmy down the street like Elvis' pelvis? Did the waiter take your order or did he recite all ten specials of the day as if he were auditioning for Steven Spielberg's new movie? Paint pictures with words. Use a fine brush, not a roller.

Show and Tell

Stories come alive when the storyteller re-creates certain moments. Get out from behind the lectern so you can "show and tell." Move from narration to action and back again. If you simply narrate a past event, it comes across as interesting. If you re-create that same event, it comes across as powerful and intriguing.

You probably relay show-and-tell stories with animation all the time. Present them as if you were in an intimate setting with a few close friends. Be natural. Whatever you do "off stage" do it "on stage." And have fun.

Stories "Move" People

Think about the last speech you heard. What do you remember? If you're like most people, you remember the stories that were told. You remember the images and sounds, most of which took place in your own imagination. There is no more receptive environment for planting the seeds of a new idea or vision than the imagination.

When you tell me something, I hear it and understand it; thus I gain knowledge about the subject. But intellectual understanding alone does not motivate people to action. Motivation comes from the Latin word *motivus*, which means to move. A strategic story contains imagery that stirs the emotions; it "moves" people.

When your story makes a logical point, knowledge converges with the motivation you've created. This brings your listeners to a new understanding and desire to take action.

Using stories strategically can help you say goodbye to sweaty palms and cottonmouth. Before you know it, you'll be having fun, making your points, and feeling your authentic power in front of an audience—just like when you're orchestrating the company's next strategic move.

Doug Stevenson is the founder and president of Story Theater International (www.storytelling-in-business.com), a speaking, training, and presentation skills consulting company based in Colorado Springs, Colorado.

• • •

PRESENTATION TALES: IT'S ABOUT THE STORY, NOT THE STORYTELLER
Jim Endicott

WEDGED IN THE APPALACHIAN Mountains in the eastern half of Tennessee is the two-century-old town of Jonesborough. As small towns go, this one is relatively rich in history, but its greatest claim to fame isn't its strategic significance in the Civil War or a famous resident. Jonesborough has distinguished itself as the epicenter of a worldwide revival in storytelling and the National Storytelling Center.

Lest you relegate the art of storytelling to small town libraries on a Saturday morning, a quick visit to their website (Storytellingcenter.com) and their Creative Applications pages will broaden your perspective considerably.

You'll discover that the same set of skills that keeps a five-year-old glued to a Sunday school teacher are not unlike the balance of spoken versus visual material (augmented by some good personal communication skills) that keep a high-profile client intently listening to your "story."

"Stories constitute the single most powerful weapon in a leader's arsenal."

Dr. Howard Gardner, Professor, Harvard University

We'd like to believe that the art of delivering a good presentation is unique. After all, we use this software called PowerPoint to capture our thoughts, our laptops and electronic projectors blast colorful images on the wall and, oh yeah, all audiences are different too—or are they?

Before you abandon the idea of storytelling for a more traditional approach to presentation delivery, let me challenge your ideas about the presentation process. If I win, you'll change for the better. If I lose, you keep doing things the way you always have.

It's About the Story, Not the Storyteller

Imagine for a moment that we took the story away from the storyteller. All the very best delivery skills and beautifully designed slides could not sweep the audience along for even a minute.

In the same way, presentations desperately need a strong underlying story that is appropriate for the audience. It needs to connect with issues, characters, and personal interests that represent common ground with the audience.

For lack of a compelling story, many presentations have died a slow and agonizing death. Here are some of the key components of effective storytelling.

Strong Opening Statement (Opening Chapter)

In the opening moments of a presentation, an audience will make a quick determination whether the presentation they are about to sit through is about them, the presenter, or the presenter's prowess with the software and technology.

We use the opening moments of a presentation to create clear relevance to an audience, often through a well-rehearsed personal story or challenge statement that engages not only their minds, but hearts as well. *Practice this critical time until it flows like water.*

A good start will also help you through the initial moments of nervousness as you get your bearings with the room and your audience.

Smooth Topic Transitions (Chapter Transitions)

All the topics of a presentation should paint a clear path toward the promises made in your opening comments regarding how this presentation relates to them. When there is little connectivity between subtopics, we run the risk of losing momentum in a presentation or, even worse, our audience's interest.

When rehearsing your presentation, work on how you transition between presentation subtopics so a thread of the storyline is carried through to the next area.

Subtopics of a presentation break up a long and lengthy single topic delivery like chapters in a book break up the storyline into more palatable packages of thought.

Well-Orchestrated and Rehearsed Conclusion (Strong Ending)

Far too often, presentations appear to end not because there is a clear conclusion, but rather it seems the presenter ran out of slides, time, or both. A storyteller works hard so his or her audiences understand the moral of the story.

If the whole point of the story is not clearly understood, a good storyteller would be hard-pressed to consider the day a success. Yet many presenters fly through the end of their presentations with little regard for a crisp, well-rehearsed conclusion.

Spend 30 percent of your practice time working on the opening and closing five-to-eight minutes of your presentation. Pull all the pieces together so the audience understands the main points behind your presentation. If your time is cut short, never compromise the time for your closing comments.

Abbreviate the depth of description in the middle of the presentation if necessary, but never the conclusion.

Graphics Aren't the Story

The pictures in a book are not the story, only a graphical set of supporting images that add greater depth to the spoken word. The pictures create emotion and connection (right-brain imagery) between the audience and storyline. Show them the same old pictures in every story and they will quickly lose their impact. In the same way, using the same stock PowerPoint template and clip art is a fast track to mediocrity.

Imagine if the storyteller simply held up the book and expected the audience to squint and read the pages for themselves. Text-intensive PowerPoint presentations seem to ask the very same thing from their audiences. Just like a children's book has unique design considerations for the medium, presentation graphics also require unique considerations that center around saying less with more graphically oriented supporting images.

The Illustrated Story

One thing's for sure, storytellers use their entire body to communicate a story. Their passion is reflected in how their eyes connect with the audience and "invite" them to participate.

Eye contact with a senior staff member or potential client is no less critical. That's why reading off cue cards or turning and reading from a projected presentation screen are usually the kisses of death for making any kind of relational connection.

A good presenter, like a good storyteller, orchestrates physical distance to create emphasis and greater relational connections. When you are making a key point or telling a personal story that supports your presentation, a step or two toward your audience will raise their attention level and give those words more impact.

But don't overuse that sacred delivery space or it, too, will lose its importance.

The evidence is painfully clear: Many presenters today fail to effectively connect in a meaningful way with their hopeful audiences. Their overly structured delivery, supported by gratuitous use of text and graphics on slides, leave them and their audiences wondering if things could ever change.

I would suggest that we could all benefit from a trip to Jonesborough, even for a day, because our biggest obstacles as presenters are not the technology, software, or audience—it's the prevailing paradigms we've associated with presenting that hold back average presenters from being truly great.

Jim Endicott is president of Distinction Communication Inc. (www.distinction-services.com), a Newberg, Oregon, consulting firm specializing in message development, presentation design, and delivery skills coaching.

10

Tuning the Speaking Instruments

BODY LANGUAGE, VOCAL TECHNIQUES, AND EYE CONTACT

Being an effective presenter isn't just about creating good speaking scripts or designing impactful PowerPoint slides. It's as much about mastering the "how" of stand-up delivery as it is the "what" of developing presentations content.

Understanding how body language, vocal techniques, and eye contact contribute to audience perception of your message is essential to taking your presentation skills to the next level. Even if you're delivering more of your presentations via webinar, where participants usually can't see you, you'll still need to ensure you use your voice with maximum effectiveness, since it's the primary conduit of communication.

This chapter features a collection of our best expert tips and advice for fine-tuning those speaking "instruments" to ensure the quality of your delivery matches the quality of your content.

• • •

AH, UM, ER . . . HOW TO ELIMINATE YOUR SPEAKING TICS
Lisa B. Marshall

A S THE SHOW HOST for the podcast, *The Public Speaker's Quick and Dirty Tips for Improving Your Communication Skills*, I regularly receive questions from my listeners. Perhaps the most commonly asked question is one like this:

> "Most of the time I feel that I am reasonably articulate, but on occasion my sentences are sprinkled with the flavorless additives 'um,' 'uh,' and 'er.' I know it is a habit from childhood that I just can't seem to shake. Could you please help me?"

Here's my standard reply.

Although it's difficult to completely rid yourself of these "credibility killers" (for example, like, so, you know, right, uh, ah), it's pretty easy to reduce them.

The good news is that you are not alone. In fact, according to researchers, these "disfluencies" sometimes represent up to about 20 percent of "words" in everyday conversation. In fact, if you listen to Barack Obama when he is "off teleprompter" you'll notice that he struggles with this, too.

Not only are disfluencies common, but some researchers believe they serve distinct conversational purposes. In 2004, a *New York Times* article on disfluencies included the finding of psychologists Herbert Clark and Jean Fox Tree. They suggest that "uh" signals a forthcoming pause that will be short, while "um" signals a longer pause.

However, when it comes to public speaking, these pauses signal to the audience that the speaker is unprepared. Which, of course, is a bad thing.

People around the world fill pauses in their own way. My husband is a native Spanish speaker and when I was first learning and practicing Spanish I would listen closely when he was speaking with his mother. I couldn't understand why he used the word "esto" so frequently. I thought I just didn't understand. But it turns out that for Spanish speakers that's a common disfluency.

When I researched it more I found out that in Britain they say "uh," Hebrew speakers say "ehhh," and the Turks say "mmmmm." The Japanese say "eto" (eh-to) and "ano" (ah-no), Mandarin speakers "neige" (NEH-guh) and "jiege" (JEH-guh). It seems disfluencies are common among all speakers.

As a public speaking coach, I notice disfluencies the most when people are nervous or are presenting on a topic they're not comfortable with. In fact, for some people it's the only time these little buggers show up. Unfortunately, that's usually when clear and confident communication is most important.

So how can you boost your immunity to these viruses? Again, notice, I am suggesting *reduction* versus complete elimination.

Um, Like . . . Do I Have Disfluencies?

The first and most important step toward more fluent speaking is to become aware of your distracting speech habits. The fastest way to find out whether you have trouble in this area is to ask a close trusted friend or public speaking coach.

The *best* way is to record yourself. If you are comfortable with technology I suggest using free audio editing software. With this software you can see your words in audio format. Of course, you also can record your presentation rehearsal with video as well.

Once you have some sample recordings, the next step is to play them back several times. Listen specifically for your disfluences—go ahead and make of game of it. First, just list them, and then start counting them. If you are counting past three or four, you know you have a problem.

If recording seems like too much effort, just focus for one full week on listening, really listening carefully for distracters when you talk. Some experts like to suggest you put tiny "um" and "ah" stickers on your computer or cell phone to remind you to be listening. Another awareness-raising tactic is to have friends listen to you rehearse a speech and simply raise their hands every time they hear you use a disfluency.

I recently attended a session and the expert suggested wearing a rubber band around your wrist. The idea was to snap the rubber band when a disfluency occurred.

Trust me, after a week of recording and listening (or worse, a week of snapping your wrist), you'll have become acutely aware of your specific problems. And that's exactly what you need: awareness. You need to be able to hear your disfluencies in your mind before you blurt them out.

I can't stress this enough. You must be able to hear your problem or you won't be able to fix it.

How to Reduce Your Credibility Killers

If you've done your homework, you'll know when one of your credibility killers is just about to escape from your mouth. Then, all you'll need to do is to keep quiet. Of course, slowing down will also help.

I know, it's easier said than done. At first you'll have awkward pauses in your speech, but that's still far better than speech peppered with "likes" and "ums." Eventually the pauses become shorter. With time, you'll be more fluent and have fewer "ums" and "ahs."

Don't let your disfluencies kill your credibility as a presenter. It's worth it to take some time to record and listen to yourself.

Lisa B. Marshall (www.lisabmarshall.com) is a communication specialist and trainer in the areas of public speaking, conflict management, interviewing, and social media.

● ● ●

THREE LESSONS YOU CAN LEARN FROM YOUR TV WEATHERPERSON
Jim Endicott

I'VE ALWAYS GLEANED a lot of coaching fodder from TV newscasters. When they are comfortably behind their anchor desks and able to shuffle papers and keep their hands occupied, they're pretty smooth. But put them in front of their news desks to do a promo spot or a special feature, and watch their hands. They simply don't know what to do with them!

If you've ever had to speak from behind a lectern, then you've experienced the same predicament—anxious hands find nervous things to do—and make no mistake, you're sending signals of low confidence whether it's true or not.

But I want to shift gears a bit to the weather guy or gal. That spot usually comes at the end of the newscast and, depending on what they have to say, you'll either hate them or love them.

Here's what I want you to see next time you're watching the weather. They have an electronic device in their hands. You hardly know it's there, but many are masters of its use.

Somehow they are making you believe they are able to highlight temperatures, change 3D settings, switch views, and push high pressure zones out to sea with their fingertips. Although the technologies are evolving, most are using the small remote devices to advance pre-created images and animations. (Sound familiar?)

Here are three lessons that every presenter can learn from his or her local weatherperson:

1. They don't point their control devices like phaser weapons. They subtly click the button as they gesture to the screen. What is the perception? They are somehow seamlessly creating change by their spoken word. No fanfare. No stop and point or technical pauses while they explore the buttons on the remote—just smooth and seamless interaction.

Here's the lesson. If you're still using an IR remote during your presentations, ditch it for an RF device and practice its stealthy use until people forget it's in your hand.

2. They always know what's coming next because their gesture anticipates the change. If you want to fall into the category of master presenter, do the same. For example, gesture to the screen from bottom to top (while you click your remote as it rests at your side) and let your audience observe the bar chart growing from bottom to top.

Other ideas? Touch elements on screen as you click and highlight them. There are endless variations on this, but here's the point: Make your technology transparent and anticipate.

3. Their audiences are more important than storm clouds. Can you imagine a weatherperson who doesn't take his eyes off of a weather chart? He wouldn't have a job very long.

Weatherpeople never lose track of the fact that there are a few hundred thousand people behind the camera lens. And you as a presenter may momentarily create focus on the screen, but the vast majority of your interaction will be eyes-to-eyes-to eyes. Not screen to floor–to foreheads–to screen–to ceiling tiles–to screen–and then maybe to eyes.

So you have your homework. Watch your weatherperson tonight. Watch how covertly he or she uses the small touchpad to change the screen. That is precisely how skilled and practiced you need to be. Because good presentations are seamless and your technology will never be as important as the connection you make with your audience.

Jim Endicott is president of Distinction Communication Inc. (www.distinction-services.com), a Newberg, Oregon, presentations consulting firm specializing in message development, presentation design, and delivery skills coaching.

● ● ●

THE POWER OF ONE-ON-ONE EYE CONTACT
T.J. Walker

THOSE NEW TO PUBLIC speaking often wonder where they should focus their eyes when they present. Should they look to the front rows, middle rows, off to the sides, or continually scan the entire audience? It's an important question, because speakers want to come across as calm and in control during their presentations, not as jittery or anxious—which is the perception you create when your eyes are constantly darting around the room.

Three Types of Eye Contact

Presenters typically use three types of eye contact. The bottom 5 percent of speakers—those who are least effective—stare at their notes, their PowerPoint slides, or even their shoes. Anything to avoid locking eyes with the audience.

It's also not unusual to catch these speakers looking at the tops of people's heads, the clock, the floor, or studying a fully written script.

The next 94 percent use some variation of the "windshield wiper" method. They look at their audiences, but sweep their gaze back and forth from one side of the room to the other, perhaps quickly, perhaps slowly.

The wiper effect may make speakers feel that they are being inclusive, but it doesn't give any one audience member the feeling that he or she is being spoken to directly. No one audience member ever receives eye contact for more than one second because the speaker is focused on the group and not on individuals. This shotgun approach has an impersonal and somewhat scripted feel, which can lead to loss of confidence in the speaker by the audience.

On the other hand, the top 1 percent of presenters use their eyes in a way that is very different from the first two groups. *They make a point of looking at individual audience members, one at a time.*

This makes them seem comfortable, confident, authoritative, and credible—even if they are quaking inside.

The direct eye contact may only last for five or six seconds, but it is long enough for the audience member to feel a personal connection with the speaker. The skilled presenter will do this with as many people in the room as possible.

The approach also has benefits for the speaker. When he or she is zeroing in on one person at a time, it provides the feeling of having a close, personal, intimate conversation with just one other person. The result is the sensation of a powerful connection between audience members and the speaker.

Making It Natural

Learning the "one person at a time" approach is not as hard a skill to master as say, becoming a brilliant composer, but it doesn't come naturally either. It's far more natural to look at someone you are speaking to for just a few seconds and then break eye contact.

It's also natural when standing in front of people to have your eyes dart nervously back and forth across the room. So it will take some concentrated practice to master this high level of sustained eye contact.

The approach also can be used with extremely large audiences. Let's say you are speaking to a convention hall of two thousand people. You are on a stage under a spotlight and the audience is in the dark, their faces hidden from view.

Here is what you do: Pick one spot in the crowd and look right at that spot for a full thought or sentence, even though you can't really see anything. The effect on the audience will be just as powerful. The twenty or so people in that general area will feel like you are speaking directly to them.

After about six seconds, use the technique with another section of the crowd. Continue to mix it up. Be careful not to look around the room in a rigid, clockwork rotation. Instead, look at the front left, then the back left, then the middle of the room. You don't want to look mechanical or like you're a prisoner to a set pattern.

A Powerful Tool

Your eyes are a powerful tool. By looking directly at audience members for five or six seconds, you will occasionally make someone uncomfortable. That's OK. Better to make them slightly uncomfortable than to make them so comfortable they fall asleep.

Remember, you aren't being rude because you aren't singling anyone out—you are doing your best to give attention to as many people as possible. If you are speaking for twenty minutes to a room of fifty people, for example, you can give each person individualized eye contact at some point during the presentation.

In a subtle way, your eye contact also conditions listeners to be better, more attentive audience members. We have all seen presenters so focused on their PowerPoint slides or script that they wouldn't have noticed had an audience member in the first row fallen over, had a heart attack, or begun making faces at the speaker.

There is only so much presenters can do with their content to make it more compelling, but when you couple great content with great, one-on-one eye contact, the result has a more powerful effect on everyone in the room.

T.J. Walker is the CEO of Media Training Worldwide (www.mediatrainingworldwide .com), a public speaking and media training company in New York City.

• • •

USE THESE VOCAL TECHNIQUES TO SET YOURSELF APART
Tom Mucciolo and Leila Jahangiri

THE VOICE PLAYS AN important role in linking concepts to content. However, the vocal elements of your skill involve more than just speaking loud enough to be heard. Several elements of your vocal strategy can take your presentation effectiveness to another level, including proper breathing, voice projection, juxtaposition, and audience interaction.

Breathing

If you tend to move around frequently as you present, you may find yourself breathing *during* your phrases, which will allow the audience to hear you taking a breath as you speak. However, by breathing *between* phrases, you will vocalize better and the audience will not hear your intake of air. While you don't want to stand completely still, it is best to limit your movements as you present.

Sometimes you may vocalize a longer phrase, but find that you don't have enough air to complete the entire sentence. You might compensate by speaking more quickly. However, this will cause your words to run together, affecting emphasis and inflection.

The inability to sustain phrasing is due to improper breathing. Try this. Take a deep breath. If your chest expands or your shoulders rise, you are not breathing properly and the chances are that you took the deep breath though your mouth. The air normally should go into the lower abdomen, the diaphragm, nearly the pit of your stomach. Try taking the same deep breath through your nose and the air will reach your lower abdomen.

Another way to test your normal breathing pattern is by lying on the floor, face up, with a book on your stomach. Breathe easily and notice the book moving up and down. Take a deep breath and it should be easy to make the book go up. Stand up and take the same deep breath, but don't expand your chest or raise your shoulders. Your stomach should expand. That is the proper way to breathe between your phrases when speaking.

This is important for languages like English, where our major points are made at the ends of our phrases, not at the beginning. Without enough air, the voice will trail off and the audience will not hear the key part of the sentence and thus make no link to the ensuing phrase.

Pause naturally between your phrases so that you can control the momentum or timing of your presentation. Each pause gives you a chance to make eye contact, breathe, or even think. Phrasing and pausing allow for smooth transitions and more consistent delivery. It also helps eliminate the verbal fillers such as "um, uh, er, you know, OK, again" and other sounds.

Simply replace those fillers with silence, using pausing as the technique.

Power of Projection

People from all areas in the presentation room must also be able to hear every word you say. You must project your voice to the back of the room, and the better your breath control the easier this task will be. In addition, your awareness of projecting to the back will keep your head up and facing forward as often as possible.

This doesn't mean you need to yell. It simply means that the intensity of your phrases, no matter how calm or soft-spoken, must always be audible.

One way to have your voice be heard most effectively is to speak primarily to the back one-third of the audience. This will force your chin slightly higher, opening your throat and allowing your voice to gain clarity in tone, carrying a greater distance as you speak.

Juxtaposition

Juxtaposing is the vocal choice of placing the emphasis on a word that is not expected to have weight. For example, using upper case to show the stressed word, the following sentence is offered:

"I went to the big GAME."

The word "game" is emphasized, as if to differentiate it from another activity that might have been described as "big." In the English language, we tend to put emphasis on nouns and verbs, leaving adjectives and adverbs to work on their own.

However, by juxtaposing the emphasis onto the adjective, the emotional power of the sentence changes. The sentence *"I went to the BIG game"* focuses the attention on the type of game, its magnitude, importance, or meaning, as if separating this particular game from the rest.

When placing vocal emphasis on adjectives or adverbs in speech, the heart of the listener becomes more engaged. Typically, those who have English as a second language tend to use juxtaposition more naturally, which is why "accents," especially ones foreign to a region, hold a distinct advantage.

Audience Interaction

When fielding responses from the audience, make sure you repeat the question or comment so the entire group can hear it. If you fail to do this, then your discussion may make sense only to those who actually heard the question or comment in the first place.

At times you may be stumped by an audience question. While your response may be along the lines of "I don't know" or "I will get back to you on that," you may be able to ask a clarifying question in order to gain some valuable evaluation time by using one of the three "E" words: Example, Explain, or Elaborate.

When someone asks you a question for which you do not have an immediate answer, you can seek clarification, saying, "Can you give me an example?" or "Can you explain what you mean?" Finally, you can say, "Can you elaborate on that?"

If you use any of these questions, the audience member must narrow down or focus his or her question to something more meaningful to you. If still in doubt, you can always admit you don't know or say that you will find out.

In essence, audiences prefer vocal clarity in order to evaluate content. Your ability to breathe properly, project continually, juxtapose occasionally, and interact strategically will allow you to deliver the intended message more effectively.

Tom Mucciolo is president of MediaNet Inc. (www.medianet-ny.com/), a presentation skills company in New York City specializing in the design and delivery of electronic presentations. He also is a multi-published author in the presentations field and an adjunct faculty member at New York University

Dr. Leila Jahangiri is chair of the Department of Prosthodontics at New York University's College of Dentistry, a global speaker, teacher, and researcher.

11

Disaster Recovery

MANAGING CHALLENGING PRESENTATION
SITUATIONS

Regardless of how well you prepare in advance of presentations—double-checking speaking notes, putting your webinar platform or projection technology through a trial run, testing microphones, or walking the stage—odds are that sooner or later something will go wrong, often at the worst possible time.

How well you steal victory from the jaws of defeat in these trying situations has a big impact on presentation success and on your credibility as a presenter. Recover quickly—and with good humor—from missteps, audience disruptions, or technology breakdowns and your audience is put at ease. But fumble endlessly, gripe, or continue on with your presentation in a diminished state and the odds of leaving your audience with a good impression drop precipitously.

This chapter offers some proven ways to cope and recover when Mr. Murphy inevitably rears his head in your presentations room.

• • •

ACE THE Q&A BY USING THE VIPP PROCESS
Marjorie Brody

THE QUESTION-AND-ANSWER period of a presentation can end everything on a high note, or it can turn the energy way down and destroy what was a well-organized and persuasive presentation.

It is a given that you will encounter tough questions and hostile questioners. Your responses can either disarm or antagonize. Being mentally and physically prepared will help you handle those difficult questions succinctly, so they don't interrupt the flow of your presentation.

The VIPP Process

An effective approach to handling a hostile question is the following four-step process, which I call the VIPP Process.

Vent

Ask the person a question and let him or her vent. Antagonists often deliver broad condemnations of what has been presented. If you try to guess what the person is specifically upset about, you're very likely to assume incorrectly. Get the antagonist to tell you why he or she is upset. Ask a question such as: "What is it about this proposal that concerns you?"

"I" Statements

As soon as the person finishes venting, you respond with something like: "I hear what you're saying" or "I can imagine how frustrating that would be." You are acknowledging the person's views and emotions. Your empathy will take away some of his or her hostility because you are really listening.

Probe

Ask questions. Start to get to the root of the matter. "Let me ask you some specifics about the situation you are referencing" or "Would you agree that this technique would work in certain situations?" You are looking for more information or a point of concession. Once you learn enough, or the person concedes something, move to step four.

Problem Solve

When you know what the specific issue is, you can respond in any one of three ways. You can

- Disprove the person's point and restate your point;

- Agree that both his or her views and yours have merit; or

- Agree to "take it off line" (that is, discuss it later) and continue with the presentation for the sake of the group.

The goal in this process is to give the antagonist a fair hearing and to have a professional discussion about his or her concerns. This process takes the emotion out of the equation.

And Remember . . .

Before answering, listen carefully and paraphrase the question before you respond. Think before you speak! Collect yourself and your thoughts. We're conditioned that silence is bad, yet skilled negotiators know the value of a pregnant pause.

Look at the questioner while paraphrasing (you can also include the question in your answer), but be sure to look at the entire audience when answering. Remember to smile. It relaxes your audience members, letting them know you're in control and confident.

Don't tell a lie by speaking out of your area of expertise. You could call on experts in the audience when appropriate, but take back control after they have responded—be aware that an expert can easily turn into a "stage hog" if not controlled. If you don't know the answer to a question, say so and offer to find the information for the questioner.

Marjorie Brody is the head of BRODY Professional Development (www.brodypro .com) in Jenkintown, Pennsylvania, which provides training programs, executive coaching, and presentations in the area of presentations power, facilitation, and meeting effectiveness. Brody also is the author of more than twenty books and is a member of the CPAE Speaker Hall of Fame.

• • •

WHAT TO DO WHEN YOU'RE LOSING YOUR AUDIENCE
Olivia Mitchell

YOUR AUDIENCE'S ATTENTION will fade over time unless you take specific steps to keep them engaged. Although our attention span is limited, we do have the ability to refocus on a task. When you push the "attention reset button" you're giving your audience that opportunity to refocus.

So that's what you need to do when you're losing your audience. Push your audience's attention reset button. Instead of fading to near zero, your audience's attention will spring back.

Plan to push that reset button about every ten minutes. This is a practical rule of thumb that seems to work for most audiences. For example, John Medina says in his book *Brain Rules*:

> "I decided that every lecture I'd ever give would come in discrete modules. Since the ten-minute rule had been known for many years, I decided the modules would last only ten minutes."

But be aware that your audience's attention span will vary according to many factors—warmth of the room, time of day, how much sleep they had the night before, how intrinsically interested they are in the topic, and more.

Be prepared to adjust to the needs of your audience. For instance, in the morning you might plan for intervals of fifteen minutes between each attention reset. During the potentially sleepy after-lunch slot, you might decrease that to five minutes.

Ways to Push the Reset Button

1. Tell a Story

We're hardwired to listen to stories. They instantly engage us and require very little effort to stay focused. Even the sleepiest audience member will perk up when you say, "I'll tell you about a time when this happened to me. . . ."

2. Make Them Laugh

Nobody can *not pay attention* when the rest of the audience is laughing. We want to know what's funny. The critical caveat is that your humor should be relevant to your presentation's messages.

3. Make a Transition

Use transition statements as a signal to the audience that they should refocus. They may have become distracted for a couple of minutes and then found it hard to get back on track with what you're saying.

But if you make a transition statement such as, "*So that's the problem we're facing, now I'll go onto my recommendation to address it. . .*" it gives the audience a chance to get back on board.

4. Break for Q&A

The traditional method of ending your presentation with Q&A is a waste of a great way of reengaging your audience. A short Q&A session *during* your presentation is more engaging because:

- It's a change from just you talking.
- Audience members can ask you questions about what they are interested in.
- There's a live element to a Q&A session that keeps people hooked.

Build Q&A into your presentation, rather than leaving it until the end.

5. Change Something . . . Anything

We pay attention to change. You're probably not aware of the air conditioning hum running in the background, but as soon as it stops you'll notice it. Here's what you can change in your presentation:

- Change the type of visual aid you're using (for example, go from PowerPoint to a flip chart or whiteboard).
- Change the spot that you're presenting from (stage to floor, different part of stage).
- Change presenters.
- Change where people are sitting in the room.
- Change what audience members are doing (for example, from sitting down to standing up).

6. Ask Them to Talk

Allowing people to process your ideas by asking them to talk to the person sitting next to them is an excellent way of reengaging them. For example, you could ask them to share with their neighbors: "What are three things you've learned so far in this presentation?"

7. Ask Them to Write

Asking people to reflect by writing is also useful. For example, "Write down three things you'll do differently as a result of my presentation."

8. Take a Microbreak

In a longer session (anything more than fifty minutes) take a two-to-three-minute break for people to stretch their legs, use the restroom, and refresh their drinks.

A Last Warning: Be Conceptually Relevant

Don't be one of those people who tries to spice up a deadly dull presentation with cartoons or funny images that are not conceptually relevant. It looks desperate, and research by Richard Mayer (the guru of multimedia learning) shows that it harms the ability of the audience to take in your core message.

Olivia Mitchell is a presentations skill trainer with the Effective Speaking consulting company in Wellington, New Zealand, and author of the Speaking About Presenting blog (www.speakingaboutpresenting.com).

• • •

HOW TO RECOVER WHEN YOU LOSE YOUR TRAIN OF THOUGHT
Jeremey Donovan

AT THE 2012 TOASTMASTERS International Convention, I had the great fortune to attend Jock Elliot's educational session. Jock, the 2011 World Champion of Public Speaking, described his thirty-five-year competitive speaking journey, masterfully weaving storytelling and presentation tips.

Perhaps the most interesting insight I gleaned came while watching Jock when he lost his train of thought. There is actually something heartening about the fact that even world champions suffer the occasional memory lapse on stage.

When he realized what was happening, Jock paused and said, "This next part is so important that I need to read it to you." He then calmly strolled back to the lectern to glance at his notes, making an intentionally audible "hmmm . . . yes . . ." as he did so. He then took back center stage and continued enthralling his audience.

Although I was very impressed by Jock's recovery technique, I was on the fence about adopting it for myself. The issue troubling me was whether or not it had crossed the authenticity line. Everyone forgets, but you should strive to recover authentically. Surely, I was not the only one to notice it was a well-rehearsed technique.

We have all seen what not to do when speakers lose their train of thought—"I . . . ummm . . . forgot what I was about to say . . . ummm. . . ." In addition to Jock's technique, are there other ways to recover?

As fate would have it, my fellow District 53 Toastmasters and I quite randomly shared a cab to Downtown Disney with Matt Abrahams. Without knowing who Matt was, we invited him to dinner with us. It turns out that Matt was leading an educational session the next day on how to overcome your fear of public speaking. In fact, he wrote a book on the subject titled *Speaking Up Without Freaking Out*.

Based on my observation of Jock, my conversation with Matt, and excerpts from Matt's book, here is how to recover gracefully.

Method 1: Make It Look Planned

This is what Jock Elliot did by pausing, saying "This next part is so important that I need to read it to you," consulting his notes, then starting again. One key lesson here is that you should always have your notes easily accessible. I keep mine in my pocket as a safety blanket; I rarely need them, but having them there sure makes me feel good.

Method 2: Paraphrase Your Previous Content

From Matt's book: "You will have to excuse me, but I am so passionate about my topic that I sometimes get ahead of myself. Allow me to review my previous point." Nine times out of ten, retracing your steps will help you find the path forward.

Method 3: Ask Your Audience a Thought-Provoking Question

Matt's recommendation is "What seems to be the most important point so far?" I feel that this technique would work better in a presentation that is highly interactive to begin with. However, you can use this as a rhetorical question to either buy time with a long pause or to precede a review of your previous content (that is, a lead-in to Method 2).

Method 4: Review Your Overall Speaking Purpose

Every speech should have a central theme—preferably encapsulated in a three-to-twelve-word catchphrase. Repeating your theme is always welcome by your audience so a memory lapse is a reasonable time to throw it back out there.

Try It Out

Unfortunately, you are going to experience a memory lapse at some time. In fact, the older you are, the more frequently it is going to happen. However, fear of memory lapses should not prevent you from sharing your ideas with the world. If Jock Elliot can lose his train of thought, then so can I. Pick one, just one, of these methods and have it in your back pocket the next time you need it.

Jeremey Donovan is author of the book *How to Deliver a TED Talk* and an avid public speaker who writes The Speaking Sherpa blog on presentation skills topics (www.speakingsherpa.com).

● ● ●

ABOUT THE EDITOR

DAVID ZIELINSKI HAS COVERED the presentations, corporate training, and human resource fields as a journalist for more than twenty years. He is the editor of *PresentationXpert* (www .presentationxpert.com), a widely read monthly e-newsletter from TriMax Direct that provides advice on how to design and deliver high-impact presentations.

David also is a contributing writer for *The Toastmaster* magazine, the flagship publication of the international speaking association, and is a former award-winning writer for *Presentations* magazine.

INDEX

Page references followed by *fig* indicate an illustrated figure; followed by *t* indicate a table.

PresentationXpert is a community of experts and practitioners dedicated to sharing the best, most practical information about developing and delivering face-to-face and online presentations. The ability to create and deliver persuasive presentations plays a crucial role in advancing the careers and income levels of business people across disciplines.

Our mission is to help you take your presentation skills to the next level—and help your organization create a competitive edge in the process. *PresentationXpert* features these knowledge-sharing initiatives designed to keep the dialog going and information flowing:

▶ A monthly e-newsletter, *PresentationXpert*, with 150,000 readers.

▶ A Webinar Wednesdays series featuring the presentation industry's top experts providing how-to advice and insights, available both live and on-demand.

▶ An enhanced website, rich with the latest presentation tips, resources, and skill-building information.

Find us online at
presentationxpert.com

▶ A Ning online community of presentation professionals dedicated to sharing best practices and lessons learned.

These initiatives are all part of our "Xpert Thinking" program designed to share cutting-edge information and ignite discussions among industry experts and presentation professionals.

Visit **presentationxpert.com** for more information and to gain access to these programs and resources.

 Follow us on Twitter at @pxpert and #presentationxpert